Good News for Today

JOSEPH R. VENEROSO, M.M.

ORBIS BOOKS

Maryknoll, New York 10545

Copyright © 2009 by Joseph R. Veneroso, M.M.

This volume is drawn from editorials previously published in *Maryknoll* magazine.

Published by Orbis Books, Maryknoll, NY 10545-0308.

Manufactured in the United States of America.

Library of Congress Cataloging-in-Publication Data

Veneroso, Joseph R.
  Good news for today / Joseph R. Veneroso.
    p. cm.
  ISBN 978-1-57075-809-6 (pbk.)
  1. Meditations. 2. Christian life--Catholic authors. I. Title.
  BX2182.3.V45 2009
  242--dc22
                                            2008046489

Contents

Contents

Introduction

Jesus urges his followers to read the "signs of the times." That is, we are to look with the eyes of faith and the wisdom of Scripture at the events happening around us and discover in them inspiration, guidance and meaning.

If we have "eyes to see," these signs may come just as much through ordinary encounters with people in our everyday lives as they do through the larger, epic events that shape and shake our world. Jesus points no less to sparrows and mustard seeds than to cosmic cataclysms as harbingers of divine intervention. Most of the gospel stories and teachings of Jesus occur in ordinary settings. He used everyday events—a measure of flour, a lost coin, a farmer sowing seed—to convey eternal truths about the kingdom of God.

How are we to read the signs of the times today? Do not the same ordinary events in our day also convey sacred truths when seen through the eyes of faith? If today is the only time that exists or ever existed, then now is the best time for discerning the presence of God in our lives. Indeed, it is the only time.

The gospels, especially, try to free us from thinking we can only find God in one particular place or people or even religion. The God of Mount Sinai has taken flesh and now abides in a baby in a barn in Bethlehem. If we are drawn to look for God in a manger, in the marketplace, and even nailed to a cross, we can find God in our world today.

These essays and editorials were written over the course of more than twenty years and appeared in *Maryknoll* magazine.

They deal with everyday situations each family faces, as well as larger themes of justice, equality, war and peace. During that time, much has changed. The gospel offers a point of stillness in a perpetually changing world. It is my hope these essays will help people recognize God in their lives and their lives reflected in the Scriptures.

Joseph R. Veneroso, M.M.

1.

Advent / Christmas / Epiphany

GOD'S IMAGE PROBLEM

Who can forget the scene from the movie *The Ten Commandments* in which Charlton Heston, as Moses, smashes the tablets of the Law against the golden calf? The earth opened up and swallowed Edward G. Robinson and the other idolaters. Hollywood helped make this Bible story known throughout the world. Never mind that artistic liberties were often taken with the dialogue, not to mention the special effects. People got to learn about the Ten Commandments, the Bible and God and that's all that seemed to matter. Ironically, strict fundamentalists, people who take each word of the Bible literally, would argue even filming such a movie violates the first commandment, which forbids not only idolatry but also the making of images. Muslims take this injunction so seriously they permit no pictures whatsoever, not even of Mohammed much less of God, to decorate a mosque or the pages of their holy book, the Qur'an.

Of course, everyone believes the god he or she worships to be the one, true God; idolatry is what other people practice. One believer's holy icon is another's false idol. Everyone thinks his or her religion is the right one, or else why would they follow it? Catholics may feel uncomfortable when they enter a Buddhist temple and see statues of various Buddhas or a Hindu shrine with images of Krishna, Shiva, Kali or numerous other deities. Many Protestants express similar uneasiness about Catholic churches with our pantheon of statues of the Blessed Virgin and other saints.

What is an acceptable representation of divine revelation? No created thing can come close to portraying God. Still, we humans long to visualize our Creator. We want a tangible expression of the transcendent. The challenge is to do so without mistaking the symbol for the object of worship. For Christians, Jesus alone is the perfect image of the invisible God (Col. 1:15). Yet even he used verbal imagery to convey divine truths. His parables smashed preconceived notions of God and shocked listeners into rethinking their understanding of how God relates to people and how we, in turn, should relate to one another.

The Ten Commandments remain both a cornerstone of our civilization as well as a point of heated controversy in our secular, multiethnic and multi-religious society. Oddly, many who advocate the Ten Commandments being displayed publicly in government buildings have trouble naming them. Even if they were to be displayed, whose translation, let alone interpretation, would be correct? For example, which Lord's Day are we to keep holy, Saturday or Sunday? Does "Thou shalt not kill" apply also to soldiers? How about animals? And what do we do with people who take the name of the Lord in vain? Of course, to many people the Ten Commandments, whichever interpretation, stand for something more: they are a visible reminder of God's concern for us and a direct, divine guide on how we are to live. They form the cornerstone of our identity as a law-abiding nation.

Over the centuries, the Church has employed icons, frescoes, stained glass windows and statues to help people visualize the gospel message of Jesus Christ. In recent years, the Catholic media have used photography, motion pictures, videos and

DVDs to illustrate religious themes. The true measure of the success of such efforts lies not in the number of copies sold or box office receipts, but rather in the number of hearts touched and lives changed. Human lives, lived in conformity to God's will as we understand it, remain the only authentic representation of the good news.

WHAT'S A NICE GOD LIKE YOU DOING IN A PLACE LIKE THIS?

Setting up a Nativity scene, a custom begun by St. Francis of Assisi, has become a favorite part of Christmas preparations for Catholics and many Christians around the world. The dramatic story of Jesus' birth has inspired countless interpretations with Nativity sets—from gaudy plastic lawn ornaments that glow in the dark to exquisite handcrafted figurines adorning the tree at New York's Metropolitan Museum of Art.

I like to set up a hand-carved, wooden crèche I brought back from Korea. A Confucian scholar, a Buddhist monk and a Taoist priest represent the three wise men from the East; a midwife approaches with food and refreshments for the visitors while outside children prepare to fly kites; farmers and country folk carrying tools of their trade surround Jesus, Mary and Joseph, who wear the clothing of a noble family. The manger is in a traditional thatched roof barn. Viewing the Nativity scene through the eyes of another culture helps us take a fresh look at the meaning of Jesus' birth.

Unfortunately, we tend to marvel at the artist's creation rather than at creation's Artist. The Nativity scene has become so familiar that what God did in Bethlehem 2,000 years ago no longer shocks us. A crèche from Mexico, Kenya or China might charm us with cultural nuances, but we may miss the essential message: God became human; not plastic, not wooden, not marble. In our efforts to retell and celebrate the Christmas story through various media, we run the risk of sanitizing it.

Let's face it: stables stink. Moldy hay, cow dung, smelly sheep, and all. What kind of place is that for any baby to be born in, much less the Son of God? Who would look for God in a place like that, anyway? I've often looked at the Christmas crèche and wondered about the characters not portrayed. Where is the High Priest of the Temple? Where are the scribes and Pharisees, the so-called holy people? Where is the upper class of Jerusalem? Who knows? Maybe all these "respectable" people were invited, just like the shepherds. But they got to the entrance to the barn and couldn't get past the smell. Shepherds, on the other hand, were used to it. They felt right at home.

Jesus' birth in a lowly stable shows God's desire not just to be human but also to be poor. Angels announce the good news, not to priests and rulers, but to social misfits: gruff shepherds who had to be brave enough to fend off wolves but gentle enough not to spook the sheep. Shepherds were regarded as religious outcasts because their job prevented them from keeping all the commandments. The wise men? So-called pagan foreigners who used superstitious practices such as astrology yet who nonetheless found God while the religious leaders of Jerusalem missed the boat. The familiar ox and the ass recall Isaiah 1:3, "The ox knows its owner and the ass its master's crib, but my people know nothing."

The Christmas crib, no less than the cross, should shake us from our complacency. The scene is an indictment of our modern standards of judging people by their wealth, looks, youth or positions of power. The Nativity invites us to search for God in the least likely places: among the poor, the misfits, foreigners and nonbelievers. Above all, in our humanity. That is the portal through which God entered the world and through which we, in turn, enter into life with God.

AN INCONVENIENT CHRISTMAS

A while ago a co-worker asked if I knew where she could get a statue of St. Joseph. She said a friend needed it to help sell her house. Apparently some people believe burying a statue of St. Joseph upside down on the property helps unload real estate.

Where do people get such ideas? Why do some people need this sort of thing? Where does faith end and superstition begin? More importantly, where is Martin Luther when you need him? On the other hand, who am I to judge what gives spiritual comfort and encouragement to people?

Catholicism abounds in practices of dubious biblical backing. Some single women invoke St. Ann to find a husband. I admit St. Anthony helped me on more than one occasion to find something I'd lost. What is a basketball player thinking when he crosses himself before making a foul shot? Make this and I'll bless you forever, or whatever happens, thy will be done?

People want religion to speak to the demands and details of everyday life in the here and now. The difference between faith and superstition is control. If I think simply by doing a certain action or saying a specific prayer a set number of times I can control God's will or actions, then that's superstition no matter how much holy water I use or how many signs of the cross I make or Hail Marys I say. On the other hand, if I use prayers and actions to show my connection to God, to remind myself God is with me and I therefore surrender to God's will, that is an act of faith.

People may think Jesus will make their lives peaceful and prosperous. The gospels tell a different story. From the moment the Blessed Virgin conceived the Son of God in her womb, her life turned upside down. St. Joseph suspected her of infidelity and planned to divorce her (Matt. 1:19). Very pregnant, she and her husband shlepped to Bethlehem where she had to give birth in a stable. No sooner was the child born than the Holy Family fled to Egypt lest Herod's soldiers massacre the baby along with the other innocents. When Jesus was 12, his parents lost track of him for three days. His family thought he'd lost his mind when he wouldn't stop preaching long enough to eat (Mark 3:21). And of course, the image of Mary cradling the dead body of her crucified son poignantly captures the cost of discipleship. Jesus repeatedly warns his disciples to expect persecution. Christianity comes at a cost. Christ demands his followers choose between comfort and the cross.

Recently the debate over immigration has divided people of faith. Can both sides be right? From a gospel standpoint, no. The word "illegal" is a smokescreen. After all, abortion is legal. That does not make it right. As with unwanted pregnancies, people insist unwanted immigrants disrupt their lives and threaten their prosperity, and some say even the national security of the United States. Building a border fence is an admission of our failure to address the more complicated issues of badly needed immigration reform and unjust economic conditions in Mexico and other countries, which force people to come here in search of work. Criminalizing immigrants does not solve the problem.

"Whatsoever you do to the least of my brothers and sisters you do to me" (Matt. 25:40) is unambiguous. It is the standard by which God will judge us. To celebrate the birth of Christ and then ignore his teachings sets Christianity on its head and sells not our homes but our souls.

GLORIA IN EXCELSIS WAILING

Celebrating the Christmas vigil Mass for the Korean community in Queens, New York, several years ago, I was waxing eloquent, as is my wont, on the mystery of the Incarnation: the Word of God taking flesh in Christ Jesus. Suddenly, from somewhere in the middle of the congregation, a baby had the audacity to cry. Loudly. I paused mid-sentence. Embarrassed, the mother stood, bundled up her wailing infant and was slinking apologetically towards the nearest exit when I asked her to return to her seat. "A crying baby sounds more like the meaning of the first Christmas than anything I am saying," I said. No one, including me, remembers what profound message I was preaching that night. But to this day parishioners recall the time a priest saying Mass welcomed a baby crying in church.

Here is the great mystery of both life and salvation. Any newborn is a breathtaking marvel. But to think that the Creator of the universe would come to us in so small, wrinkled and vulnerable a form defies belief. That 2,000 years ago a child such as this was none other than God in the flesh boggles the mind.

Just think: God became truly human, with all our weaknesses and mortality. He had not only a body and soul like us, but had a personality, emotions and relationships. Jesus was tempted like us in every way, yet without sinning (Heb 4:15). What does this say about God? More amazing, what does it say about us? Humanity was capable of bearing divinity without melting or exploding. God was not embarrassed nor humanity overwhelmed. In the beginning God created our humanity in just such a way that it might one day be the vehicle through which God entered into creation, to breathe our air, drink our water, eat our food. In Jesus, God lived and sanctified human life from the first moment of conception to the last moment of death.

As you hold a baby in your arms, watch a toddler or sigh in desperation at the rebelliousness of your teenager, consider: Baby Jesus burped and spit up and plopped on his bottom while learning to walk. Toddler Jesus put all kinds of unsavory things into his mouth much to the consternation of his mother. Boy Jesus caused great concern to Mary and Joseph. Adult Jesus knew hunger, loneliness, fear and love. He enjoyed companionship and wept at the death of his friend. The gospels never mention Jesus worshipping in the Temple. His very being was one continual act of worship; his whole life was lived in constant communion with the Father. On the cross through Jesus God experienced what it means to live and die as a human.

Every year, Christmas sneaks up on us unawares, as if its date were a surprise. We never have enough time to send all the cards, buy and wrap all the gifts, and still trim the tree. Too many interruptions, like a baby crying. But Christmas is about the ultimate, divine interruption. When God broke into human history, a baby's cooing heralded the good news. In our busy lives, Christmas does not offer us a peaceful time for reflection. But we can encounter God in the temple of our humanness, if we but cleanse it of sin. We share with God a common vocation: becoming fully human. Most of the time we profess our belief in God. Christmas shocks us with the realization that God also believes in us.

HEAVEN: FOR CHILDREN ONLY

Each Christmas morning, one curious scene inevitably takes place in homes with small children all across the nation. Frazzled parents watch in disbelief as youngsters ignore expensive gifts and, instead, play with the discarded boxes. Oblivious to the hours Mom and Dad spent searching and triumphantly locating the hottest item for tots this season, many children prefer the shiny paper, fancy ribbons and cavernous cardboard containers. Christmas, as any uninhibited toddler will readily demonstrate, is not just about being generous givers. It's primarily about being joy-filled and grateful receivers.

Receiving graciously and with joy does not come easily to most adults. We calculate (careful not to over- or underspend on a gift), anticipate (better have an extra gift ready, just in case) and speculate (Why did they give me a present? What do they really want from me?) And we don't feel comfortable until we can reciprocate, lest we find ourselves beholding to someone. The story is told of two friends who exchanged gifts at Christmas. To avoid awkwardness, they mutually agreed to limit the cost to $50. Then they simply gave each other gift cards. One year they simply started giving each other cash. It wasn't long before they stopped giving anything.

If adults have difficulty receiving gifts from one another, is it any wonder we hardly know what to do when the gift and the giver is none other than God? How does one go about thanking God, much less reciprocating? What gift can I possibly give God for all God has given me: life, creation, health, family, friends, and, of course, faith in Jesus, the supreme gift. The Bible describes elaborate rituals Jews performed for offering sacrifices to express thanksgiving to God. Unfortunately, we no longer have a Temple wherein to offer up a sheep or two. God, who created the universe and everything in it, has no need for the blood of a hapless ox. So how do we say "Thank you" to God? Has it ever occurred to us the most appropriate way to show appreciation would be for us to use and enjoy with childlike simplicity the gift God has given? As with gifts from family and friends, our enjoying and using gifts we have received, even if by so doing we wear them out or break them, are preferable to hiding them away in a closet.

Christmas celebrates God's gift of Jesus. The New Testament recounts the failure of many people to heed Jesus' warning that unless we become like children, we will not enter the Reign of God (Matt. 18:3) Even today, many either ignore or reject the Gift. Those who accept it we call Christians. People who enjoy the Gift so much they feel compelled to share it with others we call missioners. Just as proud parents beam with delight when children enjoy and share their presents, so too God delights in those who receive with open hands and grateful hearts and willingly share God's many gifts, the best of which is Jesus himself.

If we truly followed God's example we would give gifts to those who have no means to repay us, as parents do for children. And surely Mary and Joseph never repaid the Magi for their generosity; nor would the Magi expect it. Ideally it should be considered an honor to give a gift and a pleasant surprise to receive one. Each Christmas God invites us to learn from children how to receive without question, enjoy without guilt and share without fear. And in so doing we enter the Reign of God.

WISDOM FROM THE EAST

Gift-giving has become a major aspect, some would say headache, of Christmas. Upon reflection, more is wrong than the obvious materialism and rampant consumerism that forces shopping malls to decorate for Christmas in October. I remember reading a book years ago entitled *The Gospel in Solentiname* by Ernesto Cardenal, in which poor children on an island in Nicaragua reflected on the meaning of Christmas. One little boy said, "Christmas is the time when rich people give each other gifts."

Seen through the innocence of children and filtered through the eyes of the poor, both Christmas and the gospel take on new meaning, new urgency, and new life.

Epiphany inspired our custom of giving gifts at Christmastime. But the observation by the Nicaraguan child shows something has gone terribly wrong. The Magi did not give each other gifts of gold, frankincense and myrrh, much less buy them as the latest fad. Rather they presented their treasures to a newborn baby in an unknown family in a foreign land. To recapture the spirit of Epiphany, which is the true spirit of Christmas, we should examine what the Magi's example has to offer each of us in our quest for truth and ultimately, for God. Here are the lessons of the Magi:

Religious tolerance is a hallmark of true holiness. Holiness is not just when others see God in us but when we truly see God in others. Tolerance fosters respect for what is truly noble and good in other people's religions. Although the Magi were priests of the Zoroastrian religion in what is now Iran, God still led them to Jesus. There is no biblical evidence to suggest they returned home as converts to Judaism, much less to the as yet nonexistent Christianity.

Xenophobia, that is, hatred or suspicion of foreigners, is an affront to God. With the reminder to the Israelites that they were once strangers in a strange land, Leviticus 19:33 admonishes us not to mistreat the alien in our midst. The Magi willingly traveled across national borders in their search for the newborn king of the Jews. Joseph and Mary likewise welcomed these foreign visitors into their home (Matt. 2:11).

Anti-Semitism, that is, hatred of Jews, is un-Christian. Christians must never forget that Jesus was born to a Jewish mother, was raised as a Jew and lived a Jewish life, and indeed died as "the king of the Jews." All the apostles were Jewish. If the Magi disliked Jews, they would never have traveled to the land of Israel, nor set foot in the house of Miriam and Yousef (Mary and Joseph), much less knelt before baby Yehoshua (Jesus). So-called Christians who harbor anti-Jewish sentiments forget Jesus said, "Salvation is from the Jews" (John 4:22). By extension, the Catholic Church denounces all forms of racism as particularly egregious mortal sins.

The feast of the Epiphany celebrates the good news that the God of Israel has been revealed to us Gentiles. God did not hesitate to draw to Bethlehem persons from a different religion and ethnic background, even though they were not from among God's Chosen People. It would be presumptuous and foolish to assume God now speaks only to and through us Catholics or we have a monopoly on the truth. Such blindness prevented the

Pharisees from recognizing and accepting Jesus as the Son of God. God continues to reach out, guide and save all who seek truth with open minds and sincere hearts. Here is the lesson and lasting gift the Magi offer us.

THE SPIRIT OF THE MAGI

Two thousand years ago, priests of the Zoroastrian religion left their Persian homeland to travel to a foreign country in search of a new revelation from God. Astrologers who read the heavens for signs from God, these "wise men" as we call them, discovered a bright new star in the sky. Modern astronomers speculate perhaps the Magi saw a juxtaposition of two planets, possibly Saturn and Jupiter, forming what appeared to be a large star, in the constellation Pisces. According to their religion, Saturn, after which Saturday is named, governs the destiny of the Jews. Pisces is a water sign of birth and Jupiter is named after the king of the gods. Looking into the sky, the Magi read "Newborn king of the Jews" as clearly as we today might read a newspaper headline.

Common sense led them to seek this newborn king where else but at the royal palace in Jerusalem. Scripture tells us not only King Herod but the entire city was greatly upset by this news (Matt. 2:3) Paranoid and insecure, Herod could barely contain his alarm at the prospect a rival had been born and these foreigners heard about it even before his considerable spy network.

Their quest eventually led the Magi to the home of Joseph and Mary and the infant Jesus. Their gifts revealed they understood this child to be a king (gold), divine (frankincense) and a mortal human (myrrh). Warned in a dream to avoid Herod, they returned home by another route, yet all the richer for their encounter with what they had experienced abroad.

Missioners are the spiritual heirs of the Magi. Our faith impels us to leave home and everything that is familiar and follow the star of hope to unknown lands, keeping our hearts and minds open to the possibility God has something new and wonderful to teach us along the way. Sure we bring our "gifts" indicating just what this Jesus means to us. Common sense and planning often fail and many times our spiritual journey leads to frustration. Eventually we find God present in the least likely places, far from the Temple and palaces of Jerusalem: among refugees in war-torn Sudan; or among the isolated Aymara people high in the altiplano region of Peru and Bolivia; or in the determination of hard working laborers in Korea or migrants from the Philippines.

The spirit of the Magi also opens our eyes to recognize the face of God in people of other faiths: Buddhists, Muslims, Hindu and animists—people like us who dream of a better world where the divine spirit calls us to work for justice and peace among nations. Neither the pain of persons with AIDS in Thailand nor the humble surroundings of herdsmen in Tanzania can conceal the presence of God to people of faith. Before these—the poor, the oppressed, the downtrodden of the earth—we kneel and offer our various gifts to demonstrate we, too, recognize Emmanuel—God with us.

When the time comes for us to return to our native land, we who gave our gifts are spiritually enriched and eagerly share our good news with people back home. Of course, all Christians are called to be missioners by virtue of their baptism. Perhaps all are not called to travel abroad, but all are expected to cross barriers that separate people into "us" and "them." May the star of faith rise in your hearts and call you forward to find God in all peoples.

2.
Lent / Easter

CONNECTING GOD'S DOTS

Remember playing "connect the dots" as a kid? Half the fun was staring at a new page covered with clusters of random numbers with a few strategic lines and trying to figure out what picture may emerge. In a subtle way, it also taught us to play by the rules, keep order and carefully look around before making our next correct move.

Religion plays a similar role in our lives and in our world. Christianity, in particular, helps us make connections—connections we didn't see before—between ourselves and God and between us and the "cloud of witnesses" who came before us or who will come after us. Surely this is the "communion of saints" Christians confess in our creed. Faith assures us that out of this seeming chaos of modern life a picture will eventually emerge in time and our lives will find meaning and our world will make sense.

Conversely, sin and evil are the ultimate disconnects. Sin blurs the picture and cuts us off from God, from our neighbor and from our truer selves. Evil tempts us to question the point of it all and perhaps doubt, if not the existence of God, then surely of a merciful God. Evil makes unhealthy connections and relationships which rob us of our true worth and imprison our souls. Suffering can make us feel alone in a hostile universe gone terribly awry. Yet the cross of Christ reveals suffering to be the only way we can strip off our false selves and rediscover our true self.

Every year Lent invites us to step aside from the hectic and often mindless pace of our everyday life. We needn't enter a real desert so much as to delve into the innermost sanctuary of our heart and do a little spiritual housecleaning. As uncomfortable as it may be, we take a closer look at sin in order to recognize the destructive role it plays in our lives. In addition to acknowledging the role of sin and evil in our lives, these Forty Days hold before our eyes the evil that was done to an innocent man 2,000 years ago and invite us to make the connection between Jesus' suffering and our own, as well as to what is happening right now to our brothers and sisters around the world—or even around the corner.

During Lent, as we use various prayers and practices to discipline ourselves and put our own spiritual house in order, if we fail to make a connection with people in other lands our picture will forever remain incomplete. This is where missionaries come in. We go beyond the borders imposed by politics, economics or social convention to make spiritual connections with peoples in countries other than our own. But that's just half the story. Our work isn't complete until we return to tell folks back home how they too are connected to one another as well as to people overseas. We announce that, because of the death of Jesus on the cross, everyone's suffering can have meaning; all people by virtue of their humanity—a humanity we share with the Son of God— can be connected through his Resurrection and be sanctified. As Christians "connect the dots" through their lives of faith and service, a spiritual connection develops and strengthens with our next-door neighbor as well as with people in other lands. A picture of humankind emerges more glorious than we ever dared to imagine, for it reveals nothing less than the restored image of God in which all people are made.

GOD IN OUR SHOES

More curious than mean, a 7-year-old boy gingerly slaps an ant on the sidewalk just enough to injure but not kill it. He picks up and sets the crippled creature on a nearby spider web with all the intensity of a scientist conducting research, although his quest is, admittedly, more macabre and mundane: how big a hairy monster will emerge? To his horror and delight, he sees a large arachnid scurry out of its lair and move in for the kill. Then it was off in search of the next spider web—and victim. These quasi-sadistic games come to an abrupt end after one night when he has a disturbing dream. In it, he is the ant.

If you haven't already guessed, I was that little boy. Following the nightmare, I tried to make amends by diligently searching for unfortunate insects trapped in spider webs and setting them free before they became lunch. Then one day I realized I wasn't being exactly fair to the spider who, all subjective creepiness aside, is no less a creature of God than the ant or the butterfly. Thus probably began my affinity for Franciscan spirituality and love of creation.

Several years later when I was in high school, a self-proclaimed atheist teacher (I attended public school) goaded us naïve believers. "Haven't you ever played with ants?" he asked. "You amuse yourself by putting one stone after another in its path and when you get tired or bored, you squash it. Isn't that how your God treats people?"

At first I must confess I was perturbed by his question. "There's a big difference," I finally ventured. "I didn't create those ants and I never became an ant." I guess my response made an impression because his provocative prodding stopped.

Identifying with another's plight to the point of actually

becoming one with them in their suffering lies at the heart of the Incarnation: God becoming human in Jesus. It demonstrates the very meaning of compassion: to suffer with. God bestows mercy from on high; Jesus embodies compassion while nailed to a cross. Compassion is mercy within arm's reach.

With local and international news available 24/7, it is easy to become jaded. Indeed, it's almost necessary to maintain our sanity. Who, besides God, can allow themselves to be affected by each accident, crime or calamity they hear about in our neighborhood much less half a world away? We become emotionally detached to protect ourselves from the overwhelming toll compassion inevitably takes.

Where do we draw the line? How do we decide which tragedy we will allow to affect us and which to ignore? Even if someone suffers the awful yet natural consequences of his or her actions, such as smokers getting lung cancer or drunk drivers causing accidents, a simple recognition of our common sinfulness should evoke feelings of sympathy in us, "There but for the grace of God . . ." Compassion demands involvement and, by extension, vulnerability.

Jesus on the cross is God most vulnerable. Yet it is this very act of ultimate vulnerability that is responsible for the salvation of the world. As followers of Christ, all Christians are called to compassion. We are called to "suffer with." We are called to vulnerability. We suffer with others who suffer because Jesus suffered and died for all. No ant dies without the Creator knowing. Or as Jesus put it, "No sparrow falls to the ground without the Father" (Matt. 10:29). We are worth more than sparrows. Or ants. Herein lies the good news of Lent.

IN SEARCH OF THE TRUE CROSS

As Catholics we are marked by the sign of the cross. It is the most recognizable symbol of our faith. We begin and end our prayers with it. Yet for all its familiarity, people tend to misunderstand its nature. Every disease, setback or accident cannot be labeled a cross just to make it more bearable. After all, when Jesus encountered illness, he cured it. The cross results from witnessing to our faith and cannot simply be some random misfortune.

One time, while meditating on the meaning of the cross, I wrote a reflection in which I said, "No one knows what shape the cross may take, but this we know for sure: it comes." It seems the words no sooner appeared on paper when the phone rang. It was my cardiologist. I had been having an irregular heart beat following by-pass surgery the previous year. He told me, "You need a pacemaker." After the shock wore off and resistance or protestations failed, I stoically accepted what I considered my most recent cross, an image reinforced at the hospital where a nurse drew blood and a physician's assistant strapped my arms down as I lay on a cruciform operating table.

Martyrdom complex aside, the procedure was successful and not all that unpleasant. Indeed, I felt better than I had in years. Nothing like a steady supply of blood to the brain to make one feel better and more alert. During recuperation, I got to thinking. Having to get a pacemaker may initially cause anxiety, but it can hardly be considered a cross. It's nothing less than a medical miracle, albeit manmade. Conversely, disease and old age may remind us of our mortality, but they don't result from bearing witness to Christ. Everyone faces hardships, illness and ultimately death. These hardly distinguish people as followers of Jesus.

Facing challenges and overcoming difficulties with dignity certainly build character, but they don't mean we are Christian. Even dying for a religious cause, as noble as it may initially sound, does not distinguish the martyr from the terrorist. Both may lose their lives for their faith, but the first receives the violence of the world while the latter causes even more shedding of innocent blood.

So what exactly is this cross we are to bear daily to follow Christ (Luke 9:23)?

Every day we have countless opportunities to show by word and deed that God loves everyone. That all people matter. Without exception. But living this good news publicly is risky business. Therein lies the shadow of the true cross. Associating with people on the margins like Jesus did—outcasts, foreigners, migrants and "sinners"—will likely provoke a negative reaction from respectable people in society, or government, or even from within the Church. We may lose friends and alienate family members. It may cost us our job, our security—maybe even our life.

We may be tempted to live as comfortable Christians, leaving to saints and "professionals" the unpleasant business of risking everything for the love of God and our brothers and sisters. But discipleship without cost or consequences is a delusion. On the other hand, intentionally provoking "persecution" by arbitrarily breaking rules or being obnoxious does not make us authentic Christians either, just jaywalkers for Jesus.

The true cross forces us to die to our false selves. It strips away our vain egos and defenses. It shows the world we will bear the worst it has to throw at us in order to reveal through our suffering the power and glory of God.

The true cross is out of our control.

LIFE ON THE CUTTING EDGE

Some years ago a Protestant minister at an upscale church in Washington, D.C., took an unusual sabbatical. Instead of getting an academic degree or taking professional courses to hone his ministerial skills, he decided to live anonymously among the sizable homeless population in our nation's capital.

At first he never felt so alone, insecure and vulnerable. Like other homeless people, he suffered blows to his self-esteem. Without all the "essential" conveniences of modern life, he learned to survive day by day. He had no idea where his next meal would come from or where was a relatively safe place to sleep at night. How does one keep warm? Where is a good place to bathe? Which public restrooms would let him in? What does he do if he takes sick?

He even resorted to begging in order to survive. "Normal" people on the street, even those whom he recognized as parishioners or friends, either avoided making eye-contact or looked right through him as if he were invisible. Of course he could hardly blame them, given his unkempt appearance and unpleasant odor.

Eventually, he found community and fellowship with a small cluster of homeless people who lived under a highway overpass. More than that, he found deep faith and hope such as he had never before experienced in his middle-class surroundings. People with nothing cared for each other and looked after one another. Sure there were squabbles and tensions. But for the most part these homeless people recognized their common predicament and, indeed, their common humanity. After a year of his experiment, he returned to his church a changed man, humbly mindful that he, at least, always had the luxury of going home whenever he wanted.

"Society and organized religion are like trees," he later observed. "The center may be strong, but it is dead. Life and growth happen only at the edges."

Jesus embodied this truth. God entered the physical universe on a miniscule planet in a remote corner of the Milky Way galaxy. God did not become a glorious angel, but a fragile human being, an infant even. Jesus was born on the outer fringes of the Roman Empire in an insignificant village. Just prior to his public ministry, Jesus spent 40 days not praying in the Temple of Jerusalem but fasting and undergoing temptations in the wilderness of Judea. He dined with outcasts: lepers, tax collectors and sinners. He looked at the poor, the meek and those who mourn and pronounced them "blessed" (Luke 6:20).

The brokenhearted and powerless are closest to God and see the kingdom of heaven, not because they are necessarily holier than everyone else, but because they are most vulnerable. Their vulnerability opens their eyes to the frailty of life and our utter dependence on God. This is why the bishops of Latin America challenged all Christians to make a "preferential option for the poor" and minister among the world's nobodies; not to bring God to them but to reflect back to them the God of mercy and love who chooses to dwell with them on the edge.

Lent calls us to leave our familiar comfort zone and enter our own wilderness of insecurities and vulnerabilities, so as to learn to rely not on our income or status but on God alone. Our baptism and the Cross compel us to enter into the death of Jesus by giving up our own security and power and depending totally on God, in whom alone we find true life.

THE EMPTY TOMB

When I was a high school student in the 1960s my older sister Janice was a resident assistant in a dormitory at the University of Bridgeport. That year my parents decided we would all spend Easter with Jan.

Bridgeport, Conn., was one of many U.S. cities experiencing racial unrest in those days. Although there was a Catholic church just a few blocks away from my sister's dorm, my family thought it best not to venture out for Midnight Mass. My parents and my sister retired for the night, but I was upset. This was the first time in many years I wasn't singing with the choir for Easter. I went to my room and read the gospel account of the Resurrection by candlelight.

To my surprise, I felt like I was reading it for the first time. The words seemed to glow and leap off the page, searing into my mind and heart the breathtaking news, "He is not here. He is risen."

I could not read further. It was too much to bear. I covered my face as an overwhelming peace and irrepressible joy flooded every fiber of my being. It seemed as though I were in the presence of the Risen Lord himself.

Once I caught my breath, I felt I had to share this good news. My first impulse was to wake everybody. But on second thought I realized this wasn't such a hot idea—a cranky family makes poor disciples. Then I looked out the window and saw the parishioners emerging from Mass. They shared my joy—or so I thought.

One thing immediately struck me as odd: all were walking quietly to their cars. Why weren't they laughing and dancing for joy in the streets? Why weren't they all kissing and hugging like people did in Times Square after World War II ended in Europe? After all, Jesus emerged victorious over death itself!

As I looked on in disappointment, I realized that, like me for so many years, they had dutifully attended Easter Mass without fully grasping the Easter message. Everything in the liturgy invited us to peer inside the empty tomb and ponder what had taken place. Had the corpse of Jesus been stolen as the first frightened disciples suspected? Or had he in fact risen from the dead as he said? If Christ is not risen, then our faith is in vain and our sins remain, as St. Paul says in 1 Corinthians 15:16~19 and "We are the most pitiful of all people." Coloring eggs and smelling Easter lilies remain hollow amusements unless we place ourselves at the empty tomb and decide what it means.

We priests are just as distracted, if not more so, from the main gospel message. After ordination, who has time to ponder the sacred mysteries? We have to plan our homilies, meet with the parish council, discuss things with the liturgy committee, decorate the chapel, hear confessions, train the readers and altar servers and argue with the choir director. Holy Week itself is especially draining. By the time Jesus comes forth from the tomb, we are ready to move in.

But every so often, God interrupts our plans and shatters our all-important schedules. Every now and then God forces us to stop, rest and realize what Easter is all about.

If we truly believe Christ has risen from the dead, let us not hesitate to proclaim what we believe and live what we proclaim to a world desperately in need of a reason to laugh and dance and hug.

CHRIST'S UNSETTLING PEACE

Scripture paints a rather pathetic portrait of the apostles on that Sunday morning after Jesus' death. Fearful, confused and dejected, the Eleven gathered quivering behind locked doors. Their main concern: would they be next?

Even the loyal women who remained by Jesus' side until the end went to the tomb before sunrise that Sunday morning with no idea of meeting the Risen Lord. No, they carried jars of ointment to anoint their dead Messiah's body and give him a more proper burial than the hasty disposal that took place on Friday afternoon, on the eve of the most solemn Passover Sabbath.

No one expected Jesus to actually rise bodily from the dead. When Mary Magdalene saw the tomb was empty, she feared grave robbers had stolen her master's body or perhaps that someone had moved it to another location. She sat weeping at the empty tomb and mistook Jesus for the gardener. Only when he pronounced her name could she recognize him through her grief and tears. After this encounter with the Risen Christ, she ran to tell the apostles, but they dismissed her report. She was a woman and the witness of women was not acceptable. Worse, she had once been possessed by seven demons (Mark 16:9). How could the testimony of such a person be reliable? To their credit, the writers of the gospels all have Mary Magdalene as the first person to encounter Jesus after his resurrection. They would not include such an otherwise embarrassing detail unless it was true.

On the other hand, reports of Jesus rising from the dead did not exactly fill the apostles with joy. The gospel tells us the disciples were gathered behind locked doors "for fear of the Jews" (John 20:19). Maybe they feared one Jew in particular: Jesus. After all, what kind of disciple flees in the master's greatest hour of need, much less denies knowing him three times? So when Christ suddenly appeared in their midst, their wonderment was no doubt tinged by not a little shame. They no longer felt worthy.

Jesus showed his wounds to erase any doubt he was the same man who died on the cross. Instead of a well-deserved reprimand, Jesus addressed them with the Hebrew greeting used by Jews to this day, "Shalom aleichem." Peace be with you.

But shalom means so much more than peace. It means health. It means wholeness. Spoken by one who has risen from the dead to friends who had abandoned him, it also means forgiveness and reconciliation. Christ's Easter gift to them and to us is peace: not the peace of the world that comes from destroying our enemies and must be maintained by humiliating and subjugating those who wrong us. Such peace does not last. The world cannot give the peace of Christ, but neither can it take it away.

The shalom of Christ not only heals us, it frees us from sin and death, and from our distorted images of self. It prods us repeatedly until we put down our emotional baggage once and for all. It impels a person to forgive and truly repent, not out of fear of punishment but because the joy that comes with Christ's shalom makes our reluctance and false pride seem so shallow, trivial and insignificant by comparison.

We are not followers of Christ because we are worthy. We are followers because he has called us and given us his peace. True Christians have been turned totally upside down by the peace of the Risen Christ. And we cannot rest until we share this wonderful gift with everyone in the world.

3.

The Virgin Mary and the Saints

REVOLUTIONARY WOMAN

What Middle Eastern firebrand praises God for "scattering the proud in their conceit and casting down the mighty from their thrones"? What kind of revolutionary woman would proclaim God's goodness because God "feeds the hungry and drives the rich away empty"? Who praises God for "lifting up the lowly"? None other than Miriam bat Joaquin. We know her better as the Blessed Virgin Mary.

We Catholics have grown so used to the Mary of popular piety, especially in recent centuries, we forget the gospels paint a very different portrait of her. Our statues and pictures of a delicate, fair-skinned and often blue-eyed maiden bear little resemblance to what Mary probably looked like, given the olive-colored skin, jet black hair and sparkling dark eyes of most women in the Holy Land today. And the words of the Magnificat (Luke 1:46~55) show Mary of Nazareth was hardly a quiet and passive recipient of God's grace. As the place and role of women in our Church and world are debated, we would do well to revisit what the gospels have to say about the mother of Jesus.

Mary actively participated in the birth of the Messiah, questioning the archangel's words before offering herself as God's servant. Her simple yet profound "Fiat" ("Let it be done") forever changed the course of human history, as if all creation itself held

35

its collective breath until she said yes. Her hurried journey into the hill country of Judea not only allowed her to assist her cousin Elizabeth with her own pregnancy, it conveniently got Mary away from Joseph for three months so there would be no doubt about this miraculous birth. But more important, it also retraced the path taken centuries earlier by the Ark of the Covenant during the reign of King David. The unborn baby (John the Baptist) leaping within his mother Elizabeth's womb at the sound of the pregnant Mary's voice recalls David dancing naked for joy before the Ark as he escorted it back to Jerusalem from the hill country of Judea (2 Sam. 6).

Luke was showing that, as with the Ark of the Covenant, God's presence and glory had once again visited the people, this time through the woman of Nazareth named Mary. She was the new Temple wherein the glory of the Lord dwelt.

According to the Scripture's scant account, only once is Mary favored with the appearance of an angel and that was at the very beginning at the Annunciation by the Archangel Gabriel. Even that singular event left her more troubled than comforted (Luke 1:29). Her coming trials: Joseph's suspicions about the pregnancy, the trek to Bethlehem when she was about to give birth, their exile to Egypt to escape persecution and save the baby from Herod's madness, losing the child Jesus for three days in Jerusalem, and finally his arrest, trial, torture and crucifixion—all these Mary had to endure armed with nothing but her faith. Just like us.

For all the honor and veneration Catholic and Orthodox Christianity bestow upon her, except for the beautiful prayer of the Magnificat, Mary says very little in the gospels. Still, the ongoing mission of Mary and, indeed, all Christians, is found in her final words recorded in the Gospel of John 2:5. At the wedding at Cana, Jesus performs his first miracle at her urging, changing water into wine. More important than inspiring Catholics to thereby seek her intercession, Mary directs people towards Christ and says simply, "Do whatever he tells you."

THE VIRGIN MARY'S POWER

Veneration of the Blessed Virgin Mary distinguishes the Roman Catholic Church and Eastern Orthodox Churches from most Protestant denominations. Rosaries, Miraculous medal novenas and May crownings have been a staple at most Catholic parishes for generations. Despite criticism that Marian devotions detract from worship of Jesus, the custom of honoring Mary actually predates Christianity. According to the Gospel of John, the Beloved Disciple took Mary into his care following the crucifixion of Jesus. Indeed, from the cross Jesus gave his mother to his disciple as his dying wish. If, as many biblical scholars contend, the otherwise nameless Beloved Disciple symbolizes all Christians, then reverencing the Mother of God by giving her a special place in one's life is one mark of the true disciple of Christ.

Mary was present with the apostles when the Holy Spirit produced the second Body of Christ, the Church, at Pentecost. By this St. Luke seems to be showing Mary's role not just as the mother of Jesus but also as mother of the Church.

Considering how little the Bible actually tells us about Mary, it is amazing how she continually captures the imagination of each generation of believers down through the millennia. She inspired great works of art such as Michelangelo's *Pietá*, the beautiful marble sculpture of Mary holding the lifeless body of her son, her head bowed in submission to the will of God; Schubert's sublime *Ave Maria* which remains one of the most popular pieces of classical religious music; and countless churches and cathedrals such as the gothic masterpiece of Notre Dame in Paris. But undoubtedly Mary's greatest influence remains in the way she continues to touch the lives of ordinary people of faith. It is not uncommon for the poorest hovel in Honduras to reserve a special place of honor on the makeshift wall for a magazine cutout of a picture of the Virgin Mother. Vietnamese Catholics in the United States hold elaborate processions on Marian feast days. Tanzanian Catholics wore rosaries around their necks years before it became a hip-hop fashion statement in the West.

One unique characteristic of Catholicism in recent centuries remains the belief in apparitions of the Blessed Mother in various places around the world. These, in turn, have become popular pilgrimage shrines. Three of the most famous shrines include Lourdes in France, where Our Lady appeared to St. Bernadette; Fatima in Portugal, which honors an apparition to three children and predicted the end of World War I and the fall of Russia to communism; and Guadalupe in Mexico, where Our Lady appeared to a native catechist as an Aztec princess and spoke in his native language rather than in Spanish, thus precipitating a wave of conversions to Catholicism that decades of missionary activity failed to accomplish. Far from distracting people from worshipping Jesus, such shrines clearly bring people closer to God.

I received an insight into the secret of Mary's powerful place in people's hearts while I was working in Korea. After Mass one Sunday in the southern port city of Busan, I noticed a woman standing in the parish courtyard in the pouring rain without an umbrella. Tears running down her cheeks, she was praying in front of a statue of the Virgin Mary. I approached and recognized her as a local parishioner who had lost her young son in a flash flood a week earlier. I stood by her in silence, covering her with my umbrella. After what seemed an eternity of heartfelt conversation with the Mother of God, she turned to me and said, "She understands."

ST. JOHN THE TROUBLEMAKER

The Koreans in my catechism class listened in rapt attention as I told the story of John the Baptist. When I got to his rather bizarre diet of "locusts and wild honey" (Mark 1:6), they gasped. "Disgusting!" one man said, "I can't stand honey!"

I'd forgotten that salted grasshoppers roasted in sesame oil are a delicacy in Korea. (Rather tasty, too, I might add. A little like chewy popcorn.) This episode reminded me that all Christians, like all missioners, must be aware and respectful of cultural differences if we are to grasp the true significance of biblical events and persons. This is surely true of the fiery, prophetic character of John the Baptist.

The son of Elizabeth and Zechariah of the priestly tribe of Levi, John could have followed in his father's footsteps and served as a priest in the Temple. Instead, his appearance in the Judean wilderness was a rejection of Roman-ruled Jerusalem and the whole lucrative Temple franchise, with its emphasis on ritual purity and animal sacrifice. Scholars believe John once belonged to the Essene community which separated itself from mainstream Judaism and lived an austere, celibate, communal existence in the desert as it meditated on the prophesies of Isaiah and zealously awaited the appearance of the Messiah. John's diet further distanced himself from society by showing his dependence on God alone. His rough, primitive clothing of camel hair was a far cry from the comfortable linen vestments worn by the priestly class. Then, to further infuriate the religious establishment, John had the gall to make God's forgiveness freely available to anyone who submitted to being washed in the waters of the Jordan. No Temple. No priesthood. No stipend. No animal sacrifice. Just repentance. Such effrontery threatened the very foundation of Jerusalem's economy, which depended on people's willingness to pay for animals and grains to sacrifice as expiation for their sins.

When the Temple hierarchy sent a delegation to investigate this rebel, John conferred upon them a new title: "Brood of vipers" (Matt. 3:7). They, who were used to places of honor and holding high office, knew John included them when he said: "Every tree that does not produce good fruit will be chopped down and thrown into the fire" (Luke 3:9). Nor did John shrink from publicly denouncing the sin of King Herod, who married his brother's wife. It was this last act that would ultimately cost John his life. In short, John was not afraid to make waves. He didn't just rock the boat; he capsized it. But this was to prepare people to put their faith in the One who walked on water.

John came in the spirit and thunder of Elijah to announce the old order was about to be swept away and replaced by a new and revolutionary time of universal brotherhood and sisterhood under God. Then, the most prophetic, wise and courageous thing John did was to get out of the way. He could have clung to power as his popularity grew among the people. Once he revealed Jesus, his cousin, as the true Lamb of God who takes away the sins of the world, his job was done; his mission fulfilled. He stepped aside, saying, "He must increase, I must decrease" (John 3:30).

John, whose feast day we celebrate on June 24, challenges us, as individuals and institutions, to reform and repent. He knocks down our pride and lays low our claims to privilege. Above all he shows us how to overcome addiction to power by letting go of power and letting God rule our lives.

HOW TO BECOME A SAINT

I still remember my fifth grade catechism teacher at St. Michael's church in Amsterdam, N.Y. We looked to Sister Jane Marie for all things heavenly. One day she asked our class the inevitable question, "And what do you children want to be when you grow up?" One by one my classmates answered with the usual: teacher, doctor, baseball player, nurse, firefighter. Even president. But I wanted to be something else. Something different. Something more. When she came to me, I said, "I want to be a saint."

When I didn't join in the giggling, Sister knew I was serious. My friend Larry poked me in the ribs. "Idiot! You have to die first." Sister seized the moment. "No, you have to live first to be a saint," she said. There followed an animated discussion about how one attains the kind of sainthood to which the Church calls each of its members. My quest and questions continue after fifty years. And Sister Jane de la Cross and I rekindled our friendship after so many years. We meet from time to time and compare notes on our separate yet shared spiritual journeys.

Maryknoll Bishop James E. Walsh once asked, "Is it easier to imitate a saint or be one? The missioner has this much of a choice." But what exactly is a saint? Not the officially canonized, marble statued and stained glass kind, but the flesh and blood, passions and foibles kind. You know, the human kind.

Dangerous calling, sainthood. Not just because of occupational hazards like martyrdom. After all, it's probably a lot easier dying for the faith than living for it. You die once and that's it; day-to-day living the gospel in our mundane existence lacks the drama and excitement of martyrdom. This in turn leads to the temptation to become self-righteous and holier-than-thou. Like humility, holiness eludes those who claim to have it. On the other hand, how can I convince others of my holiness if I'm not convinced of it myself? A real saint isn't preoccupied with his or her own holiness. Most living saints whom I have been blessed to know would probably be shocked and embarrassed to learn I think they are holy.

Perhaps that's the key. A saint isn't so much someone in whom everyone sees God, but someone who sees God in everyone. Most people can recognize holiness in someone like Mother Teresa of Calcutta. But I believe she is a saint, not because people saw God in her but because she saw God in people, not just the poorest of the poor but also in the powerful and the rich. Recently, her letters further convinced me of her sanctity as she confessed struggling with terrible doubt for most of her life. This is something most people can relate to. She forged ahead through the darkness despite her doubts.

Instead of wasting my time and energy trying to convince people how holy I think I am, I am challenged to reflect back to people how holy they are. And when I run into the inevitable pain-in-the-butt in whom I refuse to see any goodness let alone godliness, I chalk up this experience as just another reminder from God of just how far I still have to go on the road to holiness.

To avoid the self-bloating yeast of the Pharisees, Jesus calls us to emulate the holiness of children, who look at the world in wonder; who know they need and depend on others; and who go through life playing hide-and-seek with the Lord.

ARE WE HOLY YET?

One day, a third-grader stormed home after Sunday school, grabbed her little brother and stood him in front of a full-length mirror. Intrigued, their parents asked what she was doing and why. "Sister said we are all made in the image and likeness of God," the girl replied sternly. "Is that true?"

"That's right," her mother confirmed. "Why?"

Shaking her head, the girl said, "Well, I can see God in me and I can see God in you, but when I look at Billy I think God has a very serious image problem."

Scripture continually calls us to be holy. Not pious. Not mystical. Not even religious. Holy. What does that mean? Should we pray more and eat less? Memorize the Bible, maybe? Or does holiness come from going around doing good, like a spiritual Peace Corps Volunteer?

How do we know when we are holy?

I've met some very holy people. I felt energized in their presence. They radiated life, sometimes even as they lay dying. They made me realize I was in the presence of God. They made me want to be a better person. Many were Catholic. Others were Protestant, Jewish, Buddhist or Muslim. Some were young; others old. Some were women; others men.

Clearly, belonging to the "wrong" religion or being the "wrong" gender or race is no obstacle to holiness, anymore than belonging to the right religion automatically guarantees holiness. Jesus praised a Roman soldier for having greater faith than anyone else in Israel (Luke 7:9). Such a bold declaration surely shocked members of the Chosen People who thought just belonging to the right religion and people sufficed. I've seen outwardly religious people who try too hard to impress me with their holiness. They failed to understand that, like modesty, holiness vanishes once you flaunt it.

We should seek the authentic holiness of Jesus and not the self-centered and self-important pseudo holiness of the Pharisees. Convinced of their own righteousness and confident they could follow all 613 commandments of the Bible, the Pharisees sought to show off by contrasting their pious lives to other people's sins and faults. Thus, Jesus tells of a Pharisee who proudly thanked God he was not like other men, especially like the lowly tax collector, who, for his part, humbly admitted he was a sinner and asked God to be merciful. Jesus declares the tax collector and not the Pharisee went home right with God (Luke 18:14). This parable was doubly troubling since people respected the Pharisees and despised tax collectors.

Jesus recognized the goodness in other people despite the distortions of sin or ravages of disease. Conversely, he exposed the hypocrisy of supposedly religious people. The classic example was when they set what appeared to be a perfect trap for Jesus by asking him what was to be done with the woman caught in adultery. If Jesus upheld the Law, the woman should be stoned to death and other sinners would lose faith in Jesus. If he let her go he would be accused of breaking the Law. Jesus upholds the Law yet challenges the men who think they are sinless to cast the first stone (John 8:7).

In Christ, the image of God in which all people are created but which sin distorted has been restored and the likeness of God renewed. This was done for all people for all time. This is the good news all Christians are obligated to share with everyone in the world. This is the great paradox: the more we see God in them, the holier we become.

4.
Holiness in Ordinary Time

BECOMING CANDLES

One of my earliest and fondest childhood memories of religion involves going on shopping excursions to downtown Amsterdam, N.Y., with my Aunt Josie. She always took time out from bargain hunting to duck into a Catholic church and light a candle and offer a midday prayer. While my eyes adjusted to the cool darkness, the sweet scent of beeswax and lingering aroma of incense filled me with comforting thoughts of holiness. In the corner of the darkened church, banks upon banks of flickering red votive candles continued their silent sacrifice of praise in front of larger-than-life statues of the Sacred Heart and the Blessed Mother. I watched my aunt make her offering, light her candle, kneel and pray. I knelt beside her, mesmerized by the flames. Who knows? Perhaps that scene was the first "spark," as it were, of my ultimate vocation—not only to become a priest, but also to become a candle.

Try this experiment: ask someone to draw a picture of a candle. More likely then not, the picture will also include a flame. A candle without a flame seems incomplete. It misses the candle's purpose for existing. Yet, paradoxically, the flame is the point at which the candle ceases to exist. A candle exists to give light. But to do so it must go out of existence by being consumed by flame. Its mission in life is fulfilled by the very process of dying.

Candles play important roles in most religious celebrations. Our candles at Mass not only provide a festive touch to the Eucharistic banquet, but also serve as a reminder of early centuries when persecuted Christians met in dark, torch-lit catacombs. Candles on the altar also remind us of those Christians around the world today who still suffer for their faith in such places as North Korea, Sudan or the Middle East. The four candles of an Advent wreath anticipate the return of Christ, our light, into the world and his conquering darkness. Christmas candles celebrate Christ's birth during the darkest days of the year (at least in the Northern Hemisphere). During weddings it is becoming a tradition for the bride and groom to light a "unity candle" to symbolize the new flame born of their two lives together. The candle is lit again each year on their wedding anniversary. At baptism, babies and catechumens alike receive a lighted candle as a sign of the faith that has been passed down to them. Our Paschal Candle, lit from the new fire during the Easter Vigil and given a place of honor in the church till Pentecost and again during funerals, symbolizes Jesus himself and captures the role of Christ—and all Christians—to be light for the world (Matt. 5:14).

Just as with candles, we can only fulfill our purpose in life when we allow ourselves to be sacrificed—used up—to dispel the darkness of the world. In the Bible, darkness symbolizes ignorance of God. Christ showed us the one and only way to be light and conquer evil: through self-sacrificing love and forgiveness. As Christians we are all called to be missioners by bringing the light of Christ where the world is darkest, wherever people have yet to experience the saving power of God. We hope our example helps spread the light to others and draws them closer to God. By God's grace they will experience a moment of comfort and holiness in their lives and, who knows, maybe some of them will be inspired to become candles and help spread the light of Christ to future generations.

CALLING HEAVEN AND EARTH TO WITNESS

One famous statue of Buddha shows him seated cross-legged on a lotus blossom, one hand resting on his lap, the other hand down by his side with his index finger pointing to the ground. This hand gesture, or *mudra*, is known as "Calling the earth to witness."

Born around 563 B.C. in what is now Nepal, Siddhartha Gautama lived the pampered life of a prince. His father wanted to protect him from all the unpleasantness of life and therefore sheltered his son behind palace walls where he only saw beautiful things: flowers, birds, fountains, works of art and youthful, healthy people. Curiosity finally got the best of him one day and he ventured forth into the world. He was shocked to see a sick person, an old person, a corpse, and finally a monk. Sickness? Old age? Death? That very night he left his wife and child sleeping in the palace and set out in search of the meaning of life.

Siddhartha tried living the ascetic life of a mendicant Hindu monk and, according to legend, fasted so much he reached for his stomach and touched his spine. He gave up this extreme way and vowed to remain meditating under the Bodhi tree until he awakened to the truth of all things. After 49 days of sitting, as the morning star appeared overhead, Siddhartha became the Enlightened One, or Buddha.

Following his enlightenment Buddha, like Jesus, was subjected to various temptations by Mara, the devil. He sat serenely as the devil flung one temptation after another (wealth, power and women) at him. Having failed to shake Buddha's resolve, the devil demanded to know by what right Buddha continued to sit on that piece of earth since he had now clearly transcended the need for created things. Without saying a word, Buddha simply assumed the classic pose described above. Immediately, the elephant upon which the devil was riding knelt in homage before the Enlightened One, sending the Tempter tumbling to the ground.

"Calling the earth to witness" was Buddha's answer to the charge that religious people had no business meddling in worldly affairs. Buddha's gesture declared that, because he had attained enlightenment sitting upon the earth, created matter supported him and participated in his enlightenment. It's not that spiritual people become secular but rather that the secular world is to become spiritual.

For Christians, the life and especially the death and resurrection of Jesus have cosmic implications. Gospel accounts of angelic hosts, guiding stars, earthquakes and eclipses of the sun, whether historical or dramatic embellishments, underscore the basic belief that when God became human in Jesus, all the universe was affected.

The atoms, molecules and elements that gave flesh to the Word of God came from this earth. The Incarnation not only declares humanity worthy to bear the divinity of Jesus, but also, by extension, reconsecrates the entire natural world that sustains humanity. Jesus, fully human and fully divine, drank water, ate food and wore clothing—all from this earth. We breathe the same air, literally, that Jesus breathed. His bodily Resurrection, after which he ate fish in the presence of his disciples, calls heaven and earth to witness that all creation participates in the saving work of God. His bodily Ascension into heaven consummates the wedding between the physical and spiritual worlds.

The revelation of Jesus Christ is not limited to the human race. Creation deserves the same reverence we bestow on other sacraments that bear witness to God's presence and grace.

THE BATTLE TO SAVE THE ENVIRONMENT

Throughout the school year, a sign above the blackboard on the wall of my 10th-grade classroom bore the famous quote by the poet philosopher George Santayana, "Those who cannot remember the past are condemned to repeat it." That stark prophecy instilled a sense of urgency in our young minds: ignore history at your peril.

I remember Mr. Bill Aninger, our history teacher, pointing out the tragic irony about the battle of New Orleans being fought—and lost by the British—a full two weeks after the Treaty of Ghent had already ended the War of 1812. Such was the slow and sorry state of communications in the nineteenth century. "How sad," I thought, "to fight and die in a battle already lost." Are we now condemned to repeating history?

These days, instant communications mark the beginning of the twenty-first century. Today's 10th graders text message their homies in modern shorthand: "OMG Gr8! C u. TTYL. (Just in case you can't figure out the cybercode, that's: "Oh my God! Great! See you. Talk to you later.") Gone are the days when soldiers used homing pigeons to get news back from the front. Today our men and women serving in the armed forces on foreign battlefields daily e-mail loved ones back home. Bloggers post and debate opposing viewpoints from around the globe. Cable and satellite TV offers up-to-the-minute news 24/7. Besides being used for talking, our cell phones can download maps and photos as well as the latest news. GPS (Global Positioning System) devices use satellites to locate us and give us the precise directions to any place anytime. If anything, we now suffer from information overload. Much of the so-called "information" on the Internet is blatantly false. There is so much out there, it can't all be of equal importance and truth.

Above the din, a stark reality and imminent crisis emerge. The limited resources of our planet cannot possibly sustain increasing demands for fuel, food, water and air. This is our so-called "carbon footprint": the amount of greenhouse gases, or carbon dioxide, our life and existence adds to the environment and contributes to global warming. A Google search of environmental concerns reveals a startling similarity to dire situations around the world. Deserts are expanding across Asia, Africa, and even the western United States. As the holes in the ozone layer widen, polar icecaps are melting. Ocean levels are rising. Animal species are in danger of going extinct. Air pollution caused from unregulated industry and car exhaust damage health with lung and heart diseases, which lead to early deaths. Contaminated food products cause birth defects and cancers. The sobering list goes on and on.

But, unlike the hapless British soldiers in New Orleans who, for want of up-to-date information, gave their lives in a cause already lost, we do not lack for facts and information. The very survival of our planet is at risk.

We know this, but do we have the will to do something about it before it is too late? Can we combine forces and resources with people, businesses and governments around the world to save the environment? With St. Francis of Assisi's Canticle of the Sun as our prayer, are we willing to simplify our lifestyle in order to fulfill Christ's command to "preach the good news to *all creation*" (Mark 16:15)? Or by ignoring the facts and forgetting the past, are we condemning future generations to repeat history and fight futile battles in a war already lost?

EARTH'S RIGHT TO LIFE

Imagine the excitement if a space probe to Mars sent back pictures of a single blade of grass or, better, an ant. The implications would be mind-boggling. The possibility of life on other planets, especially on our closest neighbors in this solar system, has always intrigued us and furnished us with countless sci-fi movies and books. We long for assurance that we are not alone in this vast emptiness of space and that some intelligent life "out there" may be even trying to contact us. Of course, Hollywood delights in reminding us that space aliens may not necessarily be our friends or have our best interests in mind.

As Christians, we believe an Intelligent Life is indeed trying to communicate with us and does have our best interests in mind. But not just from "out there." Our Creator communicates to us through all creation, through the atom no less than through a super nova. "The heavens declare the glory of God," the psalmist sings. "All the earth proclaims God's salvation" (Ps. 19:1).

In Thailand, some years ago, loggers planned to destroy a forest to get at the hard wood. Buddhist monks, whose temple was nearby, protested but to no avail. Thailand, a devoutly Buddhist county, reveres monks. It is against the law to harm them in any way. For their part, monks believe the Buddha nature resides in all living things, including trees. So to save the forest, they hit upon a novel solution: they ordained the trees. Seeing the saffron robes of a Buddhist monk wrapped around the trunks of trees caused loggers to stop and reconsider their plans to desecrate the forest. They were not about to risk the law of karma and wind up coming back in the next life as a bug, or worse—a tree!

Sadly, a similar situation in Brazil in 2005 had a more tragic ending. Sister Dorothy Stang of the Note Dame Sisters de Namur order gave her life to protect the Amazon forests on behalf of the indigenous peoples who live there and depend upon it for their livelihood. Death threats and warnings did not deter the 73-year-old nun. One day as she walked along a forest road, gunmen hired by the logging companies blocked her path. She stood her ground, reached into her pocket and pulled out a Bible from which she began reading the Beatitudes out loud. "Blessed are the poor in spirit . . ." (Matt. 5:3). She was still reading when she turned and walked away. They opened fire, shooting her in the back and killing her instantly. Her martyrdom reminds us that all creation, and especially Earth, is holy. Her example shows that the cost of loving the Earth and defending it is high. But how can we do less? This planet was a gift from God for our mutual benefit, not to be exploited by the few to become rich at the expense of the many.

Why look to Mars for signs of life when we live on so beautiful a sacrament as Earth? Each creature—the lowly worm no less than the majestic whale—should fill us with wonder at the power and wisdom of the One who created them—and us.

For if the smallest living thing merits respect, how much more so human life, whether within the womb or wise with age? Surrounded by miracles, we should celebrate and protect God's revelation of creation. "Ecologist" and "Pro-life" are just different ways of saying, "I believe in God."

THOSE PEOPLE

M y father, who went to church just five times a year, com-
plained about only one thing following the Second
Vatican Council. Not Mass in the vernacular, not the
priest facing the people, not even moving the tabernacle to a side
altar. No, his concern was more visceral.

Our Italian-American parish had a custom during Christmas
Midnight Mass, a custom no doubt followed in other ethnic
parishes. The life-size crèche was set up with all the major fig-
ures, except, of course, for Baby Jesus, who was up on the altar
with a veil over him. When the priest intoned, "Glory to God in
the highest," the Mass stopped, much to the chagrin of liturgical
purists. The choir would start singing the classic Italian carol *Tu
Scendi Dalle Stelle* (You Descended from the Stars) and the
priest, in solemn procession, would then uncover the Baby Jesus
and bear him down the center altar aisle toward the crèche. I
recall being deeply moved as row after row of parishioners fell to
their knees when the Infant passed. Only after Jesus was placed
in the manger did the choir continue with the rest of the Gloria.

One year, however, the pastor tried something new. Instead of
bearing the Baby Jesus himself, he gave that honor to a little boy
from the parish. Worse, he was Puerto Rican. My father was
livid. "That's the role of the priest, not t*hose* people."

"Dad," I tried to reason, "20 years ago we were *those* people."

"What are you talking about?" he said, truly confused and
offended. "We're Italian!"

Dad's ethnic myopia, I fear, is more widespread in the Church
than we care to admit, and I'm not just talking about Italian-
American parishes. We like to pray with "our own kind" but
does our concern for others stop within our own communities?

Can we recognize, much less accept, the good news when it comes to us from outsiders, strangers, visitors and foreigners. You know, *those* people? Can we let the poor evangelize us?

This is the message of Christmas. We must not allow all the lights and decorations and busyness of the season to obscure this sublime truth: God came into the world as the universal outsider—a Jew. He was born Jewish. He was raised Jewish. He lived and died as a Jew. Jesus was born and died precisely to reveal that God calls and blesses all people. "Salvation is from the Jews" (John 4:22).

When we automatically reject "those people" as the least of our brothers and sisters, be they Puerto Rican, African American or Sicilian, we reject Christ.

Missioners travel to fields afar to celebrate this revelation and share this good news: God blesses all peoples. Of course each culture has sinful customs or practices that inhibit human development, but this doesn't mean God loves them less. As people come to experience the unconditional love of God, they are ready to truly repent, or turn their lives around. They do this not to earn the grace of God but in response to it.

Sometimes it takes a tragedy to wake us up to the truth. It took the martyrdom of four U.S. churchwomen in El Salvador in 1980 to wake Americans up to the awful reality of what was happening to tens of thousands of "those people." It took two devastating hurricanes and a tsunami to make us realize "those people" are our brothers and sisters. And it took the crucifixion of a Jew 2,000 years ago to demonstrate that whatsoever we do to one of "those people" we do to the Son of God.

STRAINING THE GNAT

Jesus criticized the Pharisees for "straining the gnat but swallowing the camel" (Matt. 23:24). Neither the gnat nor the camel is kosher for Jews to eat. To do so renders Jews ritually unclean. Jesus accused the Pharisees of arguing over particular interpretations and minutiae in the Law but losing sight of the bigger requirements of love and mercy.

Such is the case, it seems, with the Roman Catholic Church's attempt to promote a consistent pro-life stance from conception to natural death. This is the so-called "seamless garment" ethnic first articulated by the late Cardinal Joseph Bernardin. Although Church teaching is clear and unequivocal, we have failed to convince our fellow Catholics, much less people of other religions, of the sanctity of all human life.

The Church's strong opposition to abortion is well known. Every January Catholics lead protests of the 1973 Roe v. Wade Supreme Court decision legalizing abortion. Bishops threaten to excommunicate pro-choice politicians. Yet statistics show Catholic women still get abortions as much as other women do. Although many Catholics publicly disagree with the Church's opposition to the death penalty, Catholic politicians who support capital punishment do not face excommunication. Both Pope John Paul II and Pope Benedict XVI repeatedly condemned the war in Iraq, labeling it a "defeat for humanity." But otherwise faithful and loyal Catholics see no contradiction in supporting the war. Personal inconsistencies and contradictions tear the seamless garment of life apart even more. Some Catholics who oppose abortion support capital punishment, while many who oppose the war in good conscience favor legalized abortion.

The shredded seamless garment can only be repaired with

threads of compassion and understanding. It isn't enough to encourage women to carry their babies to term; mothers need pre- and postnatal care. Without adequate daycare, some women cannot work to feed and clothe their children. Children have the right to a safe environment in which to live, learn and play. Without healthcare young children suffer. Fighting for workers' rights and affordable housing and anti-discrimination laws are also pro-life positions. Our challenge is to be consistently pro-life in a society steeped in the "culture of death," as John Paul II put it.

Is it a contradiction for Catholic chaplains to accompany soldiers into battle in an unjust or unjustifiable war; or rather is this a compassionate and Christian response to an unfortunate situation over which ordinary people have no control? If so, then why not be equally understanding and compassionate and not judgmental towards women who have made the unfortunate choice to terminate their pregnancies? To be consistent, our concern for the wellbeing of others cannot stop, even when they make choices that are not in keeping with our own beliefs and values.

Perhaps Catholics can learn something from followers of the Jain religion, who are really pro-life to the extreme. Jains actually do take care to strain gnats from their drinking water—not to avoid ritual impurity, but to avoid destroying even this smallest life. For them, even taking the life of vegetables to eat is regrettable, albeit necessary. Thus, they eat with reverence, conscious of the life lost so that they might live. Although this might strike us as a bit excessive, the lesson is clear: respect for life begins with the smallest and most vulnerable, but it is not consistent or complete unless it includes respect for all living things—even the lives of our enemies. In this regard, we in the West have far to go and many camels to swallow.

SAVING THE GLOBAL VILLAGE

The tall, slim Maasai warrior struck a majestic pose for a photo that graced the cover of *National Geographic* several decades ago. What made the picture memorable wasn't the customary red cloth draped over his shoulder as proof he formally came of age by killing a lion. Nor was it his deftly balancing stork-like on one leg while leaning on his spear. No, the focus of the photo was the glittering Rolex watch on his wrist.

Had we only "eyes to see" in those days, we would have recognized this odd juxtaposition of rustic and modern images as the alarming first drop in a cultural deluge about to sweep the entire world: globalization. Many of us in those days innocently hailed the emergence of a "New World Order" in which all the earth's nations and inhabitants would benefit equally or at least in proportion to their need from the quantum leap in technology, communication and transportation. We envisioned everybody in the world participating and gaining from an open and fair exchange, not just of goods and services, but more importantly, of ideas. All would be equal partners with none exploiting others. This freest of marketplaces we dubbed the Global Village.

Alas, a village is no match for an invading army of multibillion-dollar businesses and mega-corporations that operate by their own rules and beyond the reach of international law. What threatens the livelihood and cultures of so many people around the world—the Iowan farmer no less than the Maasai herdsman—is the corruption of globalization by unbridled economic greed and the destruction of local businesses, people and the environment.

Globalization gone awry underlies the Colombia coffee-grower who can easily quadruple his income and save his family from poverty simply by switching his crop to the lucrative coca leaves essential to the illegal cocaine market. Mom and Pop stores, be they grocery shops or cafes, can hardly compete with supermarkets and national chains. Billboards of plump, healthy babies encourage new mothers overseas to stop breastfeeding and use formula regardless of the lack of safe drinking water to prepare it. "Cultural imperialism" is how one Filipina Sister described foreign drug companies coming into villages with the latest medicines, sometimes untested and unsafe. The knowledge of native herbalists is forgotten as people become dependent on drugs they cannot afford. Even in the United States, we see jobs lost as goods are manufactured overseas by less than stringent safety measures for less than a living wage. Worse, people purchase and use these cheaply made goods only to learn too late they are contaminated with toxic substances.

Both the Roman Catholic Church and the United States of America are uniquely equipped to change this situation for the better. Each comprises the best of many cultures and celebrates the rich diversity other countries have to offer. The challenge is to hear the voice of those adversely affected and confront corporate greed whenever it puts profit above the welfare, health and safety of the people. Globalization can still benefit all humankind if one group does not exploit the others and if transgressors are held accountable by international courts of law. On the other hand, globalization unfettered will destroy us all. We have the right, indeed, the obligation to demand politicians and businesses protect us and all people from dangerous practices and toxic chemicals. We must act now, but time is running out, as the ticking of a Rolex watch on the wrist of a Maasai warrior ominously warns.

5.
Spirituality

OUR SPIRITUAL ADVENTURE

A sci-fi movie treated the theme of the devil tormenting people in a certain city. The main character discovered a cave behind a rented house that was the portal through which Satan entered the world from Hell. This simplistic idea of evil got me to thinking: why would the devil need a special doorway to come to earth? Couldn't he pass through walls and rocks at will? The only door the devil needs is us, for without people, it can be argued, there is no evil in the world.

Take a good look at the people around you. Think of people you've known and consider that in the book of Genesis it says that God created everyone in the divine image. Hard to believe, isn't it? Now look at the world and watch the evening news. Recall that God looked at everything he had made and saw "it was very good" (Gen. 1:31). Wars, famines, murders, corruption, earthquakes, floods.

What happened? It doesn't take a theologian to conclude some things going on are not so good and some people do not reflect the divine image in which they were made. Luckily we don't have to single-handedly shoulder the burden of repairing creation ourselves, much less of restoring the divine image in people. Jesus accomplished the latter on the cross and gives us the tools to achieve the former.

What remains is for us to absorb this truth into our lives; to "wrap our brains around it" as the current expression goes. We must let it permeate our lives and relationships so we can share it with others. Rather than concentrate on what divides people—race, religion, ethnicity or politics—we start with what we have in common.

Everyone is on a spiritual quest for a meaningful life. We all long to feel connected to one another, to ourselves, to nature, and, if we believe, to God. We have this in common with every human who ever walked the earth, from prehistoric cave dwellers to CEOs in three-piece suits; from Cleopatra's cupbearer to the annoying neighbor whose inconsiderate oak tree continually litters our yard.

Spirituality provides connectedness. Unlike religion, it's about healthy relationships rather than doctrine, rules and rituals. It allows a Christian to befriend a Buddhist, a Muslim, a Hindu, a Jew—even an atheist—without getting bogged down in theological arguments and debates, much less sectarian violence. We listen to learn. Without claiming to be the sole possessors of all truth and thus be blinded by our own conceit, we can still humbly proclaim that our faith led us to this truth: everyone is a precious child of God.

Tragically many people do not know or believe they are precious children of God. Their experience had indicated otherwise. They feel betrayed, abandoned, isolated and disposable. Intentionally or not, we may have actually contributed to their bad experiences. Our own complicity and sinfulness need not paralyze us nor excuse our inaction; rather it should spur us to make amends by building bridges of understanding between peoples and cultures, especially those different from our own. Ask people what they believe to be true, without criticism or advice as to what they should or should not think. Share your own spiritual story.

The word "devil" derives from the Greek *diabolos*, which comes from the verb "to divide." The devil divides us from one another, from ourselves and ultimately from God. By reconnecting with people and by overcoming evil with good, we undo the work of the devil and help restore goodness to creation.

A PRIEST! ARE YOU NUTS?

Any man who wants to be a priest in this day and age really ought to have his head examined. Actually, he has to. All seminaries now require psychological testing to evaluate a young man's mental readiness to begin training for the priesthood. Physical health and spiritual maturity also help determine which men are suited for the demands of a lifelong celibate commitment to Christ and the Church. Also, the sex abuse scandals may have given potential prospects second thoughts about entering the seminary. Good. Saying yes to the cross should not come easily.

Some people may caution a young man to reconsider his vocation, since the priesthood, including mandatory celibacy, is undergoing closer examination and reevaluation. While the Church may one day elect to ease up on the requirement of celibacy and return to the far more ancient practice of married clergy—after all, St. Peter was married (Matt. 8:14)—such changes often take years. However, the call from Christ remains constant; what has forever changed is the perception of priests in the public eye.

Gone are the days when admiration and adulation greeted a young man's announcement he intended to apply to enter the seminary. Nowadays he is more likely to receive looks that range from suspicion to pity. Some may question his inability to find a woman to marry or wonder how he can forgo sex, not to mention having his own children. Questioning a religious commitment is hardly new.

No doubt Zebedee was none too thrilled when his two sons suddenly abandoned the family business to hook up with some unemployed preacher and go traipsing around the Galilean countryside. When Jesus ran afoul of authorities with all that talk of the Kingdom of God and got himself arrested, tortured and executed, the disciples should have been paralyzed with fear, shame and insecurity. Perhaps they were—for a time.

But then something miraculous happened, something so powerful it overcame the stranglehold of public opinion and even the fear of death. Without money, without prestige and without Ph.D.s, these simple, erstwhile fishermen publicly witnessed to the truth. They spoke from experience and not from abstract theory. What made their message of forgiveness so compelling was that it came from the mouths of men who had themselves experienced forgiveness. Had not Peter denied Jesus three times? Did he not admit being a sinful man (Luke 5:8)? What made Peter, whom Jesus once referred to as "Satan" (Matt. 16:23), so bold as to present himself in public as the leading apostle of this new Way? There can only be one explanation: the risen Lord. Christ was so real, nothing else mattered. Not past sin. Not present shame. Not fear of persecution. Peter feeds the sheep (John 21:17) as much from his experience of forgiveness as from his faith.

Likewise Paul started out as a zealous Pharisee intent on

doing whatever he could to stamp out this new religion. He didn't convert to the New Way by studying books or engaging in debates but because he had a personal encounter with the Risen Christ. Christian faith is more than a simple, intellectual assent to a list of moral demands. It is the response of the heart as well as the head to an encounter with Christ. The Church desperately needs young people who have experienced the joy of knowing Jesus in a personal way and who are willing to spread this good news. Of course, anyone who wants to offer his or her life in service to Christ and the Church really ought to have their heads examined.

JESUS, FRODO AND US

I first encountered Frodo in 1966. I was a freshman at the State University of New York in Albany and he was the unlikely hero of J. R. R. Tolkein's trilogy, *The Lord of the Rings*. Frodo's mission was to destroy the Ring of Power and save the earth from the lord of darkness. With the war in Vietnam and protests around the country, not to mention the Cuban missile crisis and the assassinations of J. F. K., Martin Luther King, and Bobby Kennedy, who needed fiction to imagine a cosmic struggle between good and evil? When I entered the Peace Corps following graduation and flew to Korea in the winter of 1971, I felt I had entered Middle Earth. The Koreans, with their warm hospitality, sumptuous food and penchant for games, songs and laughter, were surely descendants of the Hobbits. Thatched roofs and savory smells wafting from kitchens felt like Tolkein's description of Middle Earth. Not 30 miles to the north of Seoul lay the DMZ (Demilitarized Zone) and the border of North Korea, which reminded me of the land of Mordor, where the Shadow lies.

It is no coincidence that, according to Tolkein's chronology, the Ring of Power was destroyed on March twenty-fifth. That's the day Catholics celebrate the Annunciation of the Angel Gabriel to the Virgin Mary, whose "Yes" opened the way for Jesus to conquer the Evil One once and for all. It is also no coincidence that Jesus entered the world as a tiny baby. Jesus felt tempted in the wilderness to short-circuit his mission and seize power, to "put on and use the Ring" as it were. Having shown Jesus all the kingdoms of the world, the devil said, "I will give you all this, because it has been given to me, if you but bow down and worship before me" (Luke 4:6). Hungry, thirsty and tired, Jesus must have been sorely tempted. Instead of giving in, he drew strength from Scripture and dismissed the Tempter.

Lent is our turn to enter into a spiritual wilderness and confront our own devils and temptations. By withdrawing from everyday routines and increasing our prayer, meditation and sacrifice, we can identify those areas of our life that may have fallen under the influence of shadow.

Every generation has its own war to wage against the forces of evil. Tolkein wrote as the shadow of Nazi Germany spread across Europe. Even today *The Lord of the Rings* provides a context to understand the frightening events in the world around us. Gandalf the Wizard reminds Frodo and us that we cannot choose the time in which we live. "All we have to decide is what to do with the time that is given to us."

Tolkein insisted even everyday actions have a role to play, for good or ill, in a much larger drama going on around us. Individual failures or setbacks often turn into pivotal moments from which unexpected victories emerge. Power still corrupts and ultimately destroys anyone foolish enough to use it. Mercy and forgiveness remain indispensable spiritual weapons. In the war between truth and falsehood, everyone—even the seemingly smallest, weakest and most insignificant person—might prove crucial to the triumph of good over evil.

To be sure, Christ conquered sin and death on the cross. The war is won. Yet battles remain. Facing uncertain times, we look upon the cross of Christ and draw strength in remembering, "All things work together for good for those who love God . . ." (Rom. 8:28).

RUNNING AFOUL OF THANKSGIVING

More than any other U.S. holiday, Thanksgiving calls the family together around the table for a home-cooked meal—at least in theory. Visions of Pilgrims and Native Americans sharing venison, duck and corn have given way to the de rigueur turkey, stuffing, mashed potatoes, gravy and anything else our ethnic background dictates be eaten on this day. Growing up in an Italian household, I assumed everyone else ate ravioli, artichokes, and roasted chestnuts, just as we did. Done correctly, the meal starts around 2 p.m. and continues nonstop till sometime after 7 p.m. The problem is few people these days want to cook, have the time or even know how. Also, for all its religious overtones and origins, Thanksgiving has become a secular holiday in a fast-paced culture less and less conducive to family life.

Our government gives us this holiday on the last Thursday of

November to reflect on the very things it is getting harder and harder to find, much less enjoy. Economic realities discourage some couples from having children or may force both parents to work in order to make ends meet. Conflicting and busy schedules render a regular family mealtime impractical, if not impossible. Careers compel individuals to live alone or far away from loved ones. And soaring gas prices make that trip "over the river and through the woods to Grandmother's house" unaffordable.

For some, Thanksgiving is a sad reminder of the family they do not have or the family they are no longer with. Others are only too happy to distance themselves from pesky relatives with whom they don't get along or whom they'd prefer to appreciate from a comfortable distance. The hassle of gathering for a meal, where the onus of shopping, preparing and cooking falls on the same few, seems more burden than blessing. For many, this holiday provides too many opportunities for thoughtless words and hard feelings. So what does Thanksgiving mean to us in our brave, new millennium?

At its core, Thanksgiving invites us to pause and reexamine our relationships with our families and also with food—and by extension, with the earth and its resources and those with whom we share them. Do our eating habits—not just what we eat, but how much, when and how fast—add or detract from our quality of life? Is our overabundance sustainable? Is there a more equitable way to distribute the gifts God has given us? Do our luxuries deprive others of necessities? What role does food play in our family life and social settings, on holidays and every day?

Ultimately, the greatest threat to a healthy family life in the United States is not the presence of terrorism; it's the shortage of shared time. The best antidote is not curtailed liberties, larger weapons, bigger cars and faster computers; it's spending time gathered together for a meal around the dining room table. It's not the quantity of food but the quality of our fellowship that nourishes and sustains us. Jesus took five loaves and two fish and fed 5,000 people (Luke 9:14). He willingly risked his reputation to dine openly with sinners (Mark 2:16). When it came time for him to give us an everlasting sign of his sacrificial love, he didn't ask for a monument, he gave us a meal. He told us to share with one another a piece of blessed bread and drink a sip of wine in his memory.

This simplest meal, when shared, can help us recognize God in our midst and teach us to appreciate the sacredness of food, family and friends. This is reason enough to give thanks.

OUR TURN TO RISE

Back in 1971, a primitive tribe was reportedly "discovered" living in a remote jungle area of the Philippines. At first the world reacted with excitement and fascination. Here were a primordial people living in an undisturbed Eden seemingly uncontaminated by sin, modernity or civilization. Dwelling in complete innocence, the Tasaday, as they were called, wore no clothing nor did they seem to have any concepts of anger, fighting or evil, let alone sin. The government took steps to protect the tribe from undue interference or exploitation from an influx of curious scientists and gawking tourists.

Using variations of native languages spoken elsewhere on that island, a few experts made tentative attempts at communicating with these people whom time, it seems, had forgotten. One report claimed the Tasaday had never even seen the moon because they lived in a dense, overgrown area where the forest canopy completely obscured the sky. When asked why they had never ventured to a clearing in the woods just a few miles away, they replied, "We didn't know we could."

Such innocence beguiled us. Was this what human beings must have been like before Original Sin? Would we have remained untainted by all the evils that have multiplied after the Fall? As intriguing as such speculation was, however, theologians and anthropologists alike very soon started expressing doubt as to the authenticity of this discovery. For a tribe supposedly cut off from the rest of the Philippines, let alone the rest of the world, the Tasaday bore striking resemblances, both physically and culturally, to neighboring villagers. Independent investigations revealed the Tasaday were, in fact, neither new nor different. News reporters uncovered the whole thing to be a hoax when they made an unscheduled visit to the Tasaday village and found these so-called pre-historic people sitting around wearing Tee shirts and smoking cigarettes. An unscrupulous businessman was charged with masterminding the entire scam as a way to make money from curious visitors willing to pay for a peek into Eden.

Disappointed, people still long for paradise lost, for proof of humanity's innate innocence and goodness. Our daily world of war, terrorism, suffering and injustice paints a bleaker picture of human nature. Overshadowed by sin and death and the evil people inflict on one another on a daily basis, with eyes cast down we fail to look heavenward. Maybe we didn't know we could.

Two thousand years ago, an executed criminal hung on a cross. There was nothing new or unusual about that. Crucifixion was a common occurrence in those days. It was how the Roman Empire dealt with any threat to its power. Only this time, the man resurrected from the dead. Jesus pointed the way—not back to lost innocence but forward to fullness of life. No way around death, Jesus blazed a trail through it. He provided people with a new and wonderful way of relating to God and one another. Without being overshadowed by death, he freed us to truly love and live without fear.

Yet how many of the 1.7 billion Christians in the world today live in the light of Jesus' triumph? A Francis of Assisi or Mother Teresa every 700 years will hardly convince people that Christianity offers anything new or different, much less effective.

If every Christian believed enough to dare to live Christ's truth, the world would indeed receive proof, not so much of lost innocence but of the true worth, goodness and meaning of human life. Jesus, crucified yet risen, ascended yet present, invites us to leave the shadows and gaze heavenward. We know we can.

CHRISTIAN UNITY

Fifth grade, as I recall, was rough, religiously speaking. My teacher, Mrs. Mitchell, made it even rougher, at least for us Catholics. She never lost an opportunity to point out all the things she considered wrong with Catholicism, such as our supposedly "worshiping" the Virgin Mary, or confessing our sins to a priest instead of going directly to God. And indulgences! Don't even get her started on indulgences!

Confused, angry and dejected, we Catholic kids would go for weekly released-time religious instruction and unload all our problems on Sister Jane Marie. She belonged to the Franciscan Sisters of the Atonement. The Atonement Friars and Sisters had converted en masse from the Anglican Church to Roman

Catholicism at the beginning of the twentieth century and their lasting legacy to Catholicism is the Church Unity Octave Catholics observe every January.

Sister Jane oozed ecumenism, long before I ever learned the meaning of the word. She listened patiently to our stories and grievances and encouraged us to explain our faith when we could—for example, we venerate the Virgin Mary and the saints, we do not worship them; we confess to a priest who gives us absolution in Christ's name and assures us of God's forgiveness, mercy and love. Under no circumstances were we ever to counterattack or openly criticize other faiths, especially our Protestant brothers and sisters. At all times we were to have a respectful interest in other religions.

"Our common faith in Christ," she said, "is more important than our divisions."

After almost 50 years I was able to rekindle my friendship with Sister Jane when she read one of my editorials and contacted me. I conveyed my gratitude for her strong influence in my religious upbringing. I only wish Mrs. Mitchell were still alive to benefit from Sister Jane's wisdom.

To be sure, we Roman Catholics must acknowledge our share of the blame for the current, sorry state of Christian disunity. We personally may not have caused the original cracks in the Body of Christ from the Great Schism with the Eastern Orthodox in 1054 A.D. to the Protestant Reformation, but our attitudes perpetuate our sad and deadly divisions. We cannot undo the Crusades or pretend the Inquisitions never happened, but we can take the log from our own eyes before we criticize other Christians for practices we do not like or understand. The gospel of Jesus must be our mutual measure of faithfulness.

On the night before he died, Jesus not only prayed that his

followers remain one (John 17:21), he also held up how we treat our fellow Christians as the sign of true discipleship. "By this all will know that you are my disciples, if you have love for one another" (John 13:35). Unity and love, then, are the hallmarks of true believers in Christ.

We take steps on the road to Christian unity not by boasting we are bigger, better, older or holier than other churches, but by honestly admiring what is good, noble and true in them. We can learn, for example, about solemn liturgies from the Eastern Orthodox, service and generosity from the Salvation Army, and sound, Bible-based preaching from the Baptists. Pentecostals thrive in the gifts of the Holy Spirit and Evangelicals exude great missionary zeal. Rather than regard each other as rivals, we can all advance on the way of holiness by admitting, in all humility, none of us has all the answers and that each church reflects a different aspect of the light of Christ. Loving one another despite our divisions would be good news indeed.

PRAYING ALWAYS?

Muslims pray five times a day. Before sunrise, the first call to prayer from the muezzin in the minaret awakens the faithful with the words, "Prayer is better than sleep." Christians and Jews are let off the hook. Psalm 127 assures us, "Useless is your early rising or your going late to bed, for God gives to God's beloved as they sleep."

But then Jesus tells us, " Pray always" (Luke 18:1). Not just five times a day. Always. Not just before meals or a final exam or making a foul shot in basketball. Few Catholics say grace before meals these days and fewer still bother to say grace after they've eaten. If hunger inspires us to prayer, then full stomachs, especially after a wonderful Thanksgiving dinner, induce nothing more than a "food coma," cured only by a nap or televised football game.

Praying requires a constant awareness of the presence of God. It means praying while stuck in traffic no less than after lighting a candle in a quiet church. It means inviting God into the more mundane areas of our lives, such as brushing our teeth or doing the dishes.

Perhaps it is hardest to pray when we are tired or cranky or simply too busy. But prayer need not be formal, elaborate or time consuming. Praying is much more than just saying prayers. It doesn't necessarily involve words. Indeed, mystics agree words often get in the way of true communion with God. Prayer is for our benefit. It does not inform God of something God didn't already know but rather it makes us aware of our total dependence on God. As one preface of the Mass states, "You have no need of our praise, but our desire to pray is itself your gift and makes us grow in your grace."

Prayer not only connects us to God but also to others, both living and dead. St. Paul assures us even death cannot separate us from the love of God (Rom. 8:38). Through prayer we connect with those who now rest in God, and they become spiritually present to us even as they are present to God. This is but one aspect of the mystery in the Apostles Creed we call "the communion of saints." Here lies the underpinning for the Catholic practice, not only of praying for the dead, but also on asking for the intercession of the saints.

Once we start the process of being renewed and transformed by the presence of God in our lives, we must go out and help others become aware of God in theirs. That's the essence and purpose of mission. And it is the obligation of all baptized believers.

Brother John Beeching has spent many years working among and living with Buddhist monks in Thailand. He does not convert them but rather he lets God speak to them through his actions as well as letting God speak to him through theirs. He explains his motivation this way: "Mission means falling in love with the world because you've fallen in love with God."

Prayer becomes a joy when we are content simply to be with God. Silence, too, can be prayer and can communicate on ways not possible with words. At that point, we no longer need to be told, "Pray always" any more than we need to be told "Keep breathing." From our first waking moment till our falling asleep at night, we exult and thrive and become fully alive by being with the One who means everything to us. Lovers understand.

6.
Mission

CALLING PEOPLE TO CHRIST

Have you ever been visited (some would say "annoyed") by a Jehovah's Witness intent on getting you to talk with them with their ultimate goal of getting you to change your religion? Has a Seventh-day Adventist ever buttonholed you while trying to convince you of the errors of Roman Catholicism? Have Mormons ever interrupted your nap on a Sunday afternoon with tales of Joseph Smith, Brigham Young and the Lost Tribes of Israel? If you're like most Catholics, your reaction probably ranged from anger to confusion. (Helpful hint: Jehovah's Witnesses will not pray with us, especially when we mark ourselves with the sign of the cross!)

Ironically, these same Catholics see nothing wrong with our missionaries going overseas and doing the same thing to followers of other religions. Perhaps we assume because we belong to the one true faith we have the right to run roughshod over other people's beliefs. Yet the Golden Rule ("Do unto others as you would have them do unto you"), common to every religion in the world, should prevent us from pestering, annoying and humiliating others, as we would hate people who did this to us.

The challenge facing the modern missioner is how to fulfill Jesus' command to "Go, make disciples of all nations, baptizing them in the name of the Father, and of the Son, and of the Holy Spirit" (Matt. 28:19) while respecting people's freedom of conscience and religion.

This dilemma is compounded when you realize in many countries religion and culture are inexorably intertwined. For Nepalese, Hinduism is part of who they are as a people. It's their very identity. Islam is more than another religion, it is a rich culture and total way of life. Similarly, Buddhism is as deeply ingrained in what it means to be a Thai as Catholicism is to most people in Latin America.

Just as we Catholics resent Pentecostal, Evangelical or Unification Church efforts to convert us, so too do Muslims, Buddhists, Hindus and Jews resent our efforts to convert them to Christ.

But rather than concentrate on what we perceive as our obligation to tell the rest of the world about Jesus, perhaps we should focus on everyone's right to hear the good news. Sensitive to the beliefs of people in other lands we are sent to serve, modern missioners are challenged to proclaim the gospel in such as way as to offer people an alternative rather than an ultimatum. In Nepal, where it is in fact against the law to change one's religion, Catholic missioners engage in a "dialogue of life" in which their service to people, especially those most in need, becomes a living gospel and demonstrates the heart of Christ's teachings. In Thailand, missioners accompany Buddhists on their spiritual journeys and each side finds the experience mutually enriching. True conversion becomes a daily turning of one's heart toward God.

We needn't travel abroad to be missioners and spread the good news. Just because someone is culturally Catholic or Christian doesn't mean he or she has been transformed by the gospel and spirit of Christ. How we act in times of trouble gives witness to our faith. How we treat others either glorifies or dishonors God. Above all, our joy at being followers of Christ should radiate from all we say and do. How we pray and act and treat one another should compel others to want to learn more about this Jesus whom we have chosen to follow to the ends of the earth and who has made such a difference in our lives.

CHRISTIANS HAVE NO CHOICE

Riding on the subway in Seoul, Korea, my fellow passengers and I dutifully looked away as two young men staggered aboard, dragging a third man between them. They deposited their burden on the floor right at my feet and jumped off the train just as the doors closed and the train pulled away. Nonchalantly staring forward, I tried to ascertain the condition of this unconscious inconvenience. Was he drunk? Sick? Wounded? *Dead?*

At subsequent stops, a throng of blissfully oblivious passengers miraculously stepped over or walked around him, while others absentmindedly stepped on him. A few gave me a look to suggest, "What kind of friend are you to leave your buddy on the floor like that?"

My stop was next. "God," I thought, "at times like this I almost wish I'd never heard of Jesus of Nazareth." No matter that I wasn't wearing my Roman collar. I was painfully aware of who I was and what was expected of me. When my stop arrived and the doors opened, I apologetically imposed upon two other passengers to give me a hand and help me at least get this guy out onto the platform. With much grunting, we transplanted him, still asleep, onto a bench. When a transit cop came to investigate, I explained the situation to him and then put cab fare into the pocket of the still dosing and apparently drunk dreamer.

"Do you know this guy?" the cop asked. When I said no, he looked at me incredulously, "So why are you helping him?"

"I have no choice," I said. "I am a Christian."

Sadly, this answer failed to satisfy him, so I tried a more light-hearted approach. "I'm bribing a witness for the Last Judgment." That made him more confused.

Each day, Christians confront awkward situations that demand we act as if our baptism matters. Too often we use inconvenience as an excuse to get out of doing our Christian duty. Yet, as I often point out in homilies or when teaching Sunday school, we mark ourselves with the sign of the cross, not the sign of the pillow. Christianity may offer comfort but it's not always comfortable. We do not have the luxury to pick and choose which commandments of Christ we feel like following, and when.

Unfortunately, doing the right thing at the right time does not come automatically to us. A Christian response is not second nature. We don't want to get involved. Like me, people need to goad themselves into action. Ideally we all should be able to do the Christ-like thing without even realizing it.

"Lord, when did we see you?" will be the question both the saved and the damned alike will ask at the Last Judgment (Matt. 5:37, 44). What separates these two groups is not their religions or even their prayers, but rather what they did or did not do during their lives to the least of their brothers and sisters. It doesn't even seem to matter why they did or did not do the right thing.

Jesus sets the Good Samaritan challenge before us. Will we prove ourselves neighbor to the one in need? Does faith make a difference in our daily life, or is it something we store in the closet until Sunday morning or a personal crisis shakes us out of our complacency? Regret it or not, we have heard about Jesus and we know what is required of us. So what are we going to do about it?

PAGANS AREN'T WHO THEY USED TO BE

Remember when you were a little kid and your mother coaxed you to finish all your vegetables because, "There are children starving in China"? How many of us dared express what was really on our minds? "Yeah? So send this to them!" Had I been so insolent I'd have been wearing the wooden spoon my mother always waved in the air while cooking.

Recently I recounted those maternal manipulations to a Catholic seminarian visiting from Shanghai, China. He looked at me in disbelief and laughed. China may be relatively poor but its economy is fast improving and, he pointed out, starvation and malnourishment have long gone the way of the Mao jacket.

Similarly older U.S. Catholics may recall the little alms boxes Sister used to give out for children to collect loose change during Advent or Lent for overseas missioners to "save pagan babies." The irony is that these days we have growing numbers of hungry people right here in the United States. And a modern pagan in today's world might wear a three-piece suit and work on Wall Street. In addition, many doubt the uniqueness of Christianity or the relevance of Roman Catholicism. Because of these recent developments, more and more Catholics question the urgency of sending missioners overseas, especially when we need them to spread the gospel right here. True enough.

Although the world certainly has changed rapidly in recent decades, does this mean other countries no longer need missioners or that people here in the States aren't equally deserving? Hardly. Were the entire world Catholic (a statistical improbability), there would still be a need for people of faith to be willing to live and work abroad so that both the sending and receiving countries are mutually enriched. Catholics from other countries help prevent us from being too closed in on ourselves and remind us that the Church, to be Catholic, must be universal, in outlook no less than outreach. The task remains for us to spread the gospel of Christ in more creative ways that faithfully reflect and respect these modern realities.

China is certainly different from the one that emerged following the Communist Revolution of 1949. It is even different from the China immortalized in that famous photo of one brave man blocking the tanks in Tiananmen Square during the protests of 1989. Today Shanghai and Guangjou (Canton) rival any city in the west with their ultramodern skylines, transportation and industry, not to mention young populations with a hip fashion sense. In this twenty-first century a modern missioner to China would more likely than not teach English at universities on the mainland. While he or she won't be standing on a soapbox and reciting gospel passages in Chinese to curious on-lookers, the way they conduct themselves and treat others shows them to be nothing less than people of faith.

We have learned over the years there is more than one way to proclaim the good news. Indeed, the most effective way seems to be in relating to people with respect and demonstrating to them that forgiveness, compassion and love know no distinction of race, gender, religion or political persuasion.

Changes in China and the United States hardly indicate a need to end missionary activity in either country. The human heart being what it is, people still give into the temptations of greed and power. No country has a monopoly on materialism and selfishness. But by altering our attitudes and perspectives toward people in other countries we might finally set people's feet on the road to peace.

WHAT'S MISSING FROM M SS ON?

Both Pope John Paul II and Pope Benedict XVI remind Catholics that, by virtue of our baptism, we are all called to mission. Many people associate mission with "professionals" (priests, Sisters, Brothers or even lay missioners) going to foreign lands, living among strangers, learning new languages, eating exotic foods and sometimes contracting bizarre diseases—all in order to make converts to Catholicism. If that's all there was to it, it would be so easy many more people would volunteer to do it. Mission is no longer the sole prerogative of professionals. If the Church is to succeed in its divinely mandated mission to proclaim the gospel to every nation and every creature, every Christian must play his or her part.

On almost a weekly basis we hear of horrific incidents where innocent people are robbed, beaten or struck by cars and passers-by do nothing to help. Clearly the gospel has yet to be put into practice by Christians. Truth be told, it's a lot easier to proclaim Christ overseas to a bunch of strangers than to live the gospel right in one's own home. The distance between Peoria, Illinois, and Phnom Penh, Cambodia, may be less than the distance between husbands and wives, brothers and sisters, parents and children. It may be easier to go to China and learn Cantonese than to turn to a friend or loved one and say "I'm sorry" or "I forgive you" in one's own native language. Mission begins with us.

We all need repentance, forgiveness and liberation; in a word: salvation. We need Christ to free us from unhealthy attitudes, destructive habits and oppressive customs or traditions. We need Jesus to heal our relationships. We depend upon God's grace and the Holy Spirit to exorcize racism and sexism from our hearts and institutions—including the Church. Oftentimes the task before us seems too overwhelming. "I can't do it alone," we protest. "I am with you always!" Jesus answers.

Once we have allowed ourselves to be evangelized and have begun the process or journey toward spiritual renewal we are ready to become evangelizers, bearers of the good news, both at home and abroad. Irrepressible joy impels us to share what we have found in Christ with anyone who will listen. In all humility we acknowledge that God was present in other people's lives long before our arrival. We approach other religions and cultures with reverence and respect. That does not mean we automatically bless and sanction every situation we encounter just because it is a local custom. Rather, we join people in searching for truth and justice in their lives by offering a new way of relating to God and one another. It is a way based on mutual respect and solidarity. No more exploitation. No more subjugation. No more fear. And like Christ, we might even take on ourselves the role of a slave to be with people in their hour of need. We take risks to help others. Of course we might meet with opposition from people who profit from exploiting others or destroying the environment. Sometimes even the people we seek to help might not appreciate our efforts.

If the world has failed to accept Christ, perhaps we have only ourselves to blame. Maybe we in the Church have yet to believe in the gospel enough to put it into practice, especially if it means having to change our lifestyle radically—to its root. The message of Jesus remains unchanged even after all these years; people still need to hear it. All that remains is a willingness to begin—with ourselves.

MOVABLE PRISMS OF GRACE

A Catholic missioner and a Taiwanese co-ed talked as they walked around the campus of Fu Ren Catholic University in Taipei one summer afternoon. She was curious about religion, and Catholicism in particular, but did not identify with any particular faith. She listened intently as the priest explained the differences between Catholic, Orthodox and Protestant variations of Christianity. Just then, two Mormon missionaries walked by.

"Where do they fit in?" she asked. He sighed. Before he could give her an explanation of mainline churches versus newer, so-called cults, she continued. "I got to tell you, more than anything—more than evil or natural disasters—the existence of so many churches, each claiming to be the one, true church, each criticizing the others, convinces me there is no God."

For a while they walked in silence, partly because there was not much the priest could say to counter her observation. It was sad, but true. The roses and geraniums in full bloom that lined the walkway offered a refreshing respite from the murky waters of theological discussion. The two literally stopped to smell the roses. "My favorite flower is lilacs," she said. Here, at last, was something they could agree on.

"Imagine if the world were filled with just one kind of flower," he said. "Lilacs, even, or maybe just daises, for example."

"Ugh! That would be terribly . . ." She caught herself. "You're pretty good at this," she chuckled.

"Comes with experience," he admitted.

Part of her point remains valid, however. The wide range and diversity of different religions or denominations of Christianity need not be a scandal, but the way we treat one another and regard other religions certainly is. Why criticize a cactus for not being a redwood tree? Or a pine for not being a palm? Every plant, tree and flower evolved in response to its particular environment, yet all are warmed by the same sun, albeit to different degrees. So it is with humans and our differing expressions of faith and religion. No, I don't believe all religions are equal, but more than theological argument, only one's life bears witness to the authenticity of one's faith.

Sunlight and rain symbolize God's grace which falls "on the good and the bad alike" (Matt. 5:45), but sin can obscure the light just like clouds hide the sun. People are born into very different circumstances. Unjust situations prevent some people from reaching their fullest potential as sons and daughters of God. Religions help people, not simply to cope, but to find the strength and will they need to live life to the fullest. Our God is the God of liberation, who "set us free from Egypt, that place of slavery." Insofar as our religion frees us from sin and enslavement, it is the true religion of the one, true God.

Missioners travel to places where people may not yet have heard of Jesus or realized they are children of God. We act as movable prisms of grace, letting the Son shine through us, imperfections and all, to foster faith. To paraphrase Mother Teresa, we give people an experience of God's love; after that, it's up to them how they choose to worship. We challenge the powerful to form a just relationship with God by treating the poor, the oppressed and the outcast with compassion. Thus, as the Church takes root in various ways around the world, each reflects its particular situation and, God willing, people learn to appreciate and celebrate the diversity of God's beautiful garden called Earth.

7.

Scripture

OUR TRULY DANGEROUS BIBLE

Newcomers to my weekly Bible study group inevitably ask, "Is the Bible true?" Aware that I am paraphrasing Pontius Pilate but still wanting them to think and not just memorize, I usually counter with, "What do you mean by 'true'? Factual? Historical? Scientific?"

Totally bewildered, they usually reply, "Yes!"

To help them appreciate the power and range of intentionally symbolic language, since all language, spoken or written, is symbolic by definition, I have them think about a common experience. "Has anyone here ever seen a beautiful sunset?" Invariably every hand goes up. "No, you haven't!" I contend. "That's scientifically impossible."

Initial puzzled looks one by one give way to illumination when I point out the sun does not set; the earth turns. Yet, Galileo and Copernicus notwithstanding, not even a scientist says, "What a spectacular earthturn!" Facts sometimes obscure truth. We speak from our perspective and viewpoint. Symbolic or poetic language expresses human perceptions and experiences in ways dry facts or strict scientific language cannot.

Another case in point: which expression comes closer to the truth, saying, "I am very, very sad" or "My heart is broken"? The former sentence may be true but the latter conveys pain, even though a quick X-ray of my heart would reveal it is not, in fact, actually broken.

Not intended to be a science book, our Bible is a collection of scrolls written by various authors over some 15 centuries. The writers used legends, prophecy, history, psalms, gospels and epistles to inspire and instruct the Chosen People and to remind them of God's promises and commandments. When we approach the Bible for study, as we open it up to a particular book or passage, our first question should not be "Is it true?" but rather, "What kind of literature is this?" And "What did this mean in past times?" "What was the author attempting to communicate?" And "What was the situation of the audience for whom this work was intended?" And, or course, "How do the Church and biblical scholars interpret this?" Only then can we get to the all-important question of what this means for us today in our particular place and time.

Muslims believe their holy book, the Qur'an, is a word-for-word revelation given directly from Allah in Arabic to the Prophet Mohammed, who simply took down dictation. It can therefore never be changed or edited. Jews and Christians, on the other hand, believe our Bible is the inspired Word of God, but written mostly in Hebrew and Greek by humans and therefore open to various interpretations. This has led to differing versions of the Bible, separate religions and denominations, not to mention wars.

New translations of the Bible certainly yield new insights into the authors' intended meaning, but these in turn can result in even more divisions and misunderstandings. Christians, in particular, must also pass any understanding they have of Scripture through the filter of the gospel, which of necessity takes pride of place among all other inspired books.

Without sufficient prayer and study, we run the risk of distorting God's word by misusing select passages to justify our prejudices or preconceived notions. Even a correct reading and living out of the Bible could get you into trouble. Jesus predicted as much. It is a truly dangerous book. Perhaps the Bible should come with a warning: read at your own risk; but ignore it to your eternal peril.

DO WE NEED A NEW GOSPEL?

Imagine the excitement if archeologists working in the Holy Land discovered a heretofore unknown gospel. Scripture scholars have long speculated about the existence of just such a scroll. Matthew's and Luke's gospels, for example, both quote verbatim from a now lost document scholars refer to as Q. In addition, the manuscripts we do have differ in translation. Often sections are missing. Hoping to clear up such misinterpretations, theologians would diligently examine any newfound texts to gain insights into exactly what Jesus meant when he said such unsettling things such as, "Love your enemy" or "Pray for those who persecute you" and "Do good to those who hate you." Maybe we would all be left off the hook with the discovery and addition of a little phrase such as "Love your enemy, *unless you're at war*," and "Pray for those who persecute you, *and then get even*," or "Do good to those who hate you, *after you defeat them*."

For good or ill, such a gospel has not yet been found. It's just as well. We have enough difficulty just trying to live out the Sermon on the Mount as it is. Our success rate is not encouraging. We Christians are stuck with the uncompromising words and actions of Jesus as recorded by the four Evangelists, Matthew, Mark, Luke and John.

The late Pope John Paul II was equally uncompromising in his efforts to bring Christ's message of peace and life to a world addicted to power, obsessed with amassing material wealth and willing to use violent means to impose one's will on others. Like a voice crying in the wilderness, the pope consistently decried the "culture of death" that contaminates modern society from abortion, to capital punishment, to war. In unequivocal terms he labeled the war in Iraq a "defeat for humanity." Ironically, the very ones who accuse others of being "Cafeteria Catholics" themselves pick and choose which Church teachings they'll obey when it comes to war.

Politicians may rationalize their support for war and couch their terms in noble-sounding patriotic slogans, but they cannot justify their positions based on anything Jesus said. We must never hide our moral responsibilities as Christians behind the American flag. Patriotism must never be used as an excuse to neglect our gospel duties. Our faith in Christ compels us to speak out when we see a flagrant violation or injustice perpetrated in our name. Of course, it is often easier to criticize others than to do our duty as Christians and Americans. Participating in a protest march on Washington to end the war and bring our troops home may be more dramatic and personally satisfying, but the real and harder work for peace begins in our own hearts and homes. Anyone can claim to love an enemy thousands of miles away rather than have to deal with an obnoxious neighbor or annoying relative.

For all our religious differences, every Christian denomination reminds its followers that we live in a global village and we are our brothers' and sisters' keepers. Whatever we do in violence or hatred toward others, no matter where in the world they live, we do to Christ. To create a world of justice and peace that truly protects life, absent the discovery of a new gospel, we will just have to do our best to apply the gospel we already have.

GOSPEL: LOVE IT AND LIVE IT

Many years ago when I was fresh out of college, I was waiting to catch a bus in New York City's Port Authority Terminal. Suddenly a young, female devotee of the Hare Krishna sect approached me. She offered me—for a nominal donation—a copy of their holy book, the *Bhagavad Gita as It Is*. The rather thick book had sacred Sanskrit verses, translations and interpretations, all illustrated by colorful pictures of Lord Krishna, usually portrayed with blue, that is, divine, skin. Having studied comparative religions, including Hinduism, in college, I sought to dismiss her by explaining I had already read parts of her bible. Her answer impressed me and remains with me to this day. "If you really want to know about the Gita you can't learn it just from a book," she said in all sincerity. "You must come and see how we live." She then gave me a business card with an address on it and invited me to attend one of the weekly vegetarian feasts the Hare Krishnas throw for spiritual seekers, such as myself.

Although I never took her up on her kind offer, her invitation got me to thinking. I wonder how many Christians could say to strangers, "If you want to know what the gospel is all about, you can't get it from just reading the Bible. You must come and see how we live." Yet this is precisely our responsibility as followers of Jesus: to believe in him and his gospel enough to live it. We can never convince others of the truth of our faith just by debating theology with them, much less by simply telling them to read the Bible. Winning such a debate only proves your skill as a debater, not as a believer. The most compelling way to preach the gospel is to become, in effect, living gospels. As one missioner put it: "Your life may be the only gospel some people will ever read." We must live in such a way that our lives would make no sense without Jesus.

Missioners take this one step further. The Spirit compels us to go overseas and share the peace and joy we have found in Christ with everybody in the world, especially the poor, the sick, the lonely and the oppressed. But we also need people overseas, even from different religions, to challenge us and enrich our faith with their understanding and experiences of the divine. Instead of arguing with Protestants, why not encourage one another to remove from our individual lives and Churches whatever does not reflect gospel values? We can better climb the spiritual mountain together as companions not rivals.

When we enter into dialogue with people of other religions or with those who even might share our Catholic faith, we should do so with the attitude of first removing the log from our own eyes before criticizing them for the speck in theirs (Matt. 7:5). Lord knows we each have things in our personal and communal lives that do not reflect gospel values. We must admit we sometimes do or say things that may actually turn people away from the Church, or worse, from God. The scary part is, the gospel is only as true and authentic as our ability to believe and live it. Alone we can do nothing. Together we can translate our lives into a community of faith where those who wish to learn about the good news of Jesus Christ need only "come and see."

ST. PAUL, APOSTOLIC PAIN IN THE BUTT

St. Paul was arguably the greatest missioner who ever lived. From reading his many epistles it is also clear he was a pain in the butt. Apparently these two are not mutually exclusive. Some of his outdated ideas about women being silent in church (1 Cor. 13:34) and keeping their heads covered (1 Cor. 11:6) would get him kicked off most parish councils today; still, we should not be too hasty in dismissing him, his ideas and his actions in helping form the early Church. Paul's mission methods remain progressive even by our contemporary standards. Most of all, his conviction that the message of Jesus was intended for all people helped turn Christianity into a world religion. He still has a lot to teach us.

He traveled extensively from Jerusalem through Syria, Greece, Turkey and southern Italy up to Rome, spreading the good news about the saving death and glorious resurrection of Jesus Christ. But he stayed in one area only long enough to gather a viable community of believers. Rather than impose a one-church-fits-all structure based upon the way things were organized back in Jerusalem, he encouraged a variety of ministries according to the gifts of the Holy Spirit and different structures according to the needs of the local community. He wrote prolific letters that inspired and admonished Christians not only in his time, but also throughout the ages.

Paul did not let the fact that he was a late bloomer among the Apostles stop him from confronting the head of the Apostles, Peter himself, for treating Jewish and Gentile converts differently (Gal. 2:11). In fact, it was this showdown with Peter, in which Paul prevailed, that settled the argument about whether Gentiles had to become Jews first.

Using "inculturation" two millennia before the word existed, Paul turned the Athenians' penchant for novel theological debate into an opportunity to proclaim that the Unknown God they honored was none other than the loving, forgiving God revealed by Jesus (Acts 17:23).

When he got into hot water with the locals, as he often did, Paul did not hesitate to invoke his Roman citizenship to escape (Acts 16:37) even though that same empire had crucified our Savior and eventually would execute Paul for disturbing the peace with his bold proclamations about Jesus.

But perhaps Paul's greatest inspiration to believers of all ages was his personal conversion story, recounted no less than three times in the New Testament. Earlier, he had zealously persecuted Christians, seeing in them a blasphemous distortion of what he considered the true faith. He was complicit in the stoning death of St. Stephen, holding the cloaks of the men involved in punishing this blasphemer. Then one day while on the road to Damascus to arrest more believers, Paul encountered the Risen Christ. This experience was so real, so powerful, so overwhelming that his life, the Church and the world forever changed. It formed the basis for Paul's belief that God saves us, not because of some good works we do, but rather "while we were still sinners" (Rom. 5:8). Henceforth he could speak forcefully and convincingly of grace, forgiveness and salvation. By the grace of God he has been forgiven. From then on, good works, for Paul, flowed as a result of one's experience of salvation and were not a means to earn God's favor. Yet for all his words and deeds, Paul eloquently reminds us of the primary importance of love in everything we say and do (1 Cor. 13).

NOTORIOUS GNOSTICS

Every Christmas or Easter you can always count on the secular media to announce yet another archeological discovery or supposedly radical theory about the Star of Bethlehem, the Shroud of Turin, the relics of the True Cross or even the identity of Jesus. The normal fare paled in comparison to what *National Geographic* did during Holy Week in 2005. They announced with great fanfare that an ancient manuscript had been discovered, translated and published. It bore the provocative title: Gospel of Judas.

Needless to say this caused quit a buzz. But the title alone raised biblical scholars' eyebrows. None of our four canonical gospels identifies its author; Catholic tradition supplied their names later. The newly discovered manuscript dates from around 180 A. D., but Judas committed suicide just hours before Jesus died. He didn't even leave behind a suicide note, let alone have time to pen his memoirs. Judas spoke Aramaic, like Jesus and the other apostles did. The manuscript is written in Coptic, the language of ancient Egypt. I am no biblical scholar, but even a cursory reading of the English translation of the 26-page document convinced me this was hardly the earth-shattering discovery its advocates claimed.

Personally I have always found the character of Judas intriguing and often wondered what really led him to betray Jesus. Unfortunately, the manuscript sheds no light on the historical Judas nor his motives, much less, as one headline hyped, "set Christianity on its head." Rather, the document portrays Judas an the indispensable collaborator with our Lord in doing the thankless task of betraying Jesus so that he might get captured and executed and Scripture thereby be fulfilled.

The Gospel of Judas is a text from one of Christianity's oldest heresies: Gnosticism. Gnostics believed creation was evil, the product of the false creator god (that is, the God of the Old Testament). Trapped inside a few select human beings was a divine spark of the one, true god. All other people were soulless. Gnostics saw no need for a savior since they denied the existence of sin. The only human fault was ignorance. Those with the divine spark received a revelation of knowledge (from the Greek *gnosis*, ergo the term) that separated them from the doomed masses.

Second-century Christianity was awash in documents, each purporting to have one saint or another as its author to lend credibility. Church Fathers sifted through these scrolls and parchments to agree on which to include in what we now call the New Testament. Most documents were excluded because they distorted the message or meaning of Jesus.

So why should we in the twenty-first century take the Gnostics and the Gospel of Judas seriously? St. Thomas Aquinas taught that heresies help us defend, define and refine our faith. Much of our Nicene and Apostles' Creeds—belief in one God, the Creator; Jesus becoming human; his suffering and dying; the physical resurrection of the body—was specifically aimed at countering Gnostic claims to the contrary.

The Gnostic Gospel of Judas compels us to re-examine our faith. Do we see creation as good and treat it with respect, if not reverence? Do we think our bodies are inferior to our souls? Do we believe all people are created in the image and likeness of God? Do we believe that the salvation offered by the Lord Jesus is available to all? In short, are we truly Christian or closet Gnostics? Our beliefs should profoundly affect how we relate to our bodies, our brothers and sisters, and all creation.

8.
Mother, Father, Family

GOD'S CO-CONSPIRATOR

Sure, the call to a religious life comes from God, but—at least in my case—God had a secret agent on earth: my mother. That's not to say she was even aware of this or in any way encouraged my becoming a priest. Far from it. As a 10th-grader, when I first informed my parents of my interest in perhaps becoming a priest, they were both horrified. They wondered where they had gone wrong. My mother was convinced if I became a priest I would starve to death. Where she got this idea from, I'll never know. It certainly wasn't from looking at the priests around us. Since ordination, my ever-expanding waistline dispelled her fears. My father, for his part, suspected someone had filled my head with this crazy idea. Little did he know that "someone" was none other than the Holy Spirit, with help from my mother.

From my earliest days, my mother nourished my mind and molded my personality by reading me stories about King Midas, cursed with his golden touch, and Mother Francis Xavier Cabrini, whose missionary heart was too big for our world. Mom strictly forbade toy guns in our house. Thus, whenever my friends and I played Cowboys and Indians, I always sided with the Indians.

She comforted me at age 5 when my pet canary died. She

explained to me that all living things eventually die in order to make room for new life and give others a chance. In some mystical way, even death was part of God's plan. She taught me to let go. With the characteristic stubbornness and bravery of her Calabrese background, she boldly stood in the breach and interceded on behalf of my sister and me whenever my father's anger flared.

The kitchen was the largest room of our house. Family and friends regularly gathered around out table. Visitors were hardly in the door when my father would ask what they wanted to drink and my mother would start putting tasty, usually homemade treats on the table. We seldom, if ever, said grace before meals but I noticed a quaint Italian custom. Should a piece of bread accidentally fall to the floor, my mother would pick it up (the five-second rule notwithstanding) and reverently kiss it.

Is it any wonder I grew up with missionary zeal, a pacifist's heart, compassion for the oppressed, solidarity with the underdog, a love for the Eucharist and a desire to make everyone feel at home around the Lord's table? Through my mother, God was preparing me both for priesthood and mission.

By the time I was ordained in 1978, you would have thought my becoming a priest was her idea. My parents went from thinking someone filled my head with crazy ideas to declaring, "That's my son, the priest!" Accepting my being a missioner overseas, however, was another matter. In weekly letters to me in Korea she reminded me, "We need priests here, too, you know." Only after my parents, at ages 71 and 72, finally visited me at my parish in Masan, Korea, and experienced the friendliness of the Korean people and the generous and warm hospitality of my parishioners and above all, how happy I was there, did my mother say, "Now I understand."

Mom passed away on December 2, 2002, at the age of 94. Her son, the priest, offered her funeral Mass, in thanksgiving for the one who not only taught me so much, but above all taught me to let go.

CALLING GOD "ABBA"

Of all the symbolic names Jesus might have chosen to express God's relationship to humans—creator, king, judge, savior, master, lord—Jesus tells us to address God by the one open to the greatest misunderstanding and misinterpretation: "Father."

Actually, Jews have been addressing God as "Father" for many centuries, long before the time of Jesus. A rabbi who used to teach in the Maryknoll School of Theology explained why Jews call God "Father" and not "Mother." According to Rabbi Asher Finkle, it was in no way to put down maternal love, but rather to distinguish between a mother's instinctive love for the infant in her womb, and a father's need to wait to demonstrate his love for his child. A baby feels enveloped by the tender love of its mother and hears her heartbeat months before it is born. A child only learns who its father is by experience. The father must prove his love and show he protects, defends and guides his children. Such was Israel's understanding of God's love, not as something instinctive that came naturally but as something learned experientially.

Unfortunately, some people have less than positive memories or experiences of and feelings towards their earthly fathers and this may impact their ability to call God "Father." Should orphans or abandoned children view God as absent or heartless? Do children of separated or divorced parents have a part-time or weekend God? Should abused children fear an angry, violent and cruel God? Would teenagers find it as awkward to talk openly with God as they might with their own fathers?

Cultures differ greatly on the role and expectations of a father. In Korea, the Confucian values dictate one's father be afforded great respect, but not necessarily love. He is expected to keep a dignified distance from his offspring. In Italian households, the father rules—but the mother reigns. I've heard Italian families referred to as "clandestine matriarchies." Irish fathers are noted for being gentle, strong and wise but are not given to open displays of emotion or affection. If each of our interpretations of what a father is differs according to our individual experiences and ethnic backgrounds, how then are we to understand God's fatherly love for us?

In his letter to the Galatians, chapter 4, verse 6, Paul writes that the Holy Spirit empowers us to join Jesus in calling God, "Abba," a term of intimacy and endearment closer to "Daddy" than to "Father." The difference is more than degree. Any healthy male can biologically sire children; only a man who listens, loves, laughs, spends time with, consoles, guides and gently corrects children proves himself worthy of the title: "Daddy."

Jesus invites us to draw closer to God, who not only created us and gave us life, or sired us, if you will, but who continually nurtures, protects and even fawns over us like a doting Dad. Jesus wants us to experience in our lives the tender, fatherly love of God.

Perhaps custom prohibits us from addressing God so informally or so familiarly as "Daddy." Nevertheless we need to rediscover and experience this intimate side of God's love if we are to be true Christians. All fathers, spiritual or physical, share a holy vocation. We are called to reflect in our lives the caring, intimacy, understanding, patience and encouragement Jesus taught us to expect from God. We are called to give people a real life experience, which comes from knowing the love of God, our heavenly Dad.

SUFFERING FOR CHRIST'S SAKE

Just prior to her death, my 94-year-old mother's health started to decline rapidly. She had always been so feisty, stubborn, and independent, it was difficult yet unavoidable to put her in a nursing home when the time came. She was growing weaker and falling a lot. Her mind, though fading, remained alert. "Why am I here?" she would ask each time I visited.

"Mom, you fell in the garden. Remember? These people want to make sure you don't fall and hurt yourself any more."

"Oh," she'd say. "OK." Then we'd talk about different things. My sister, Jan, and I were grateful she adapted so quickly to her new surroundings. Of course, at the very next visit she'd ask us, "Why am I here?" and the whole conversation would be repeated.

Then on Thanksgiving Day in 2002 it became obvious to my sister and me that Mom was slowly, gently leaving us. In less than a week and a half she passed away. If there is any such thing as a happy death, that was it. She lived a full life and then, when it was time, she peacefully died.

The death of one's mother is a singular event. She is the one through whom I entered the world. Her death brought to mind the words of St. Paul, "We make up in our bodies what is lacking in the sufferings of Christ" (Col. 1:24).

This passage always struck me as curious. What could possibly be missing from the sufferings of Christ? After all, one drop of his blood would have sufficed to save the entire human race for all ages, yet on the cross he shed all his blood for us.

As I prepared to preside at Mom's funeral and contemplated life without my mother around to love, encourage and guide me, I began to understand what St. Paul was getting at.

When God decided to enter our world in the person of Jesus, God accepted the limitations of living a finite human existence. There was only so much Jesus could experience in the span of one lifetime, and a shortened one at that. So Jesus chose the cross as the vehicle of God's grace to reveal God's presence even in the midst of unspeakable suffering, religious rejection and a tortuous death. He chose the most shameful and scandalous way to die to show that, if God could be present there on the cross, God could be with us no matter what happened to us.

Still, there was only so much Jesus could suffer in his brief life on earth. Jesus never had to bury his mother, or suffer the loss of a spouse, or weep at the death of his own child. Jesus never had to deal with terminal illness or bear the cross of old age. It's up to us, his followers, to make up in our bodies what is missing in the sufferings of Christ, to show that, no matter what, God is present in each situation. By our faith in God and hope in the resurrection, we shine the light of grace into the darkest and saddest recesses of our individual human existence. Tragedy becomes transfigured.

When we pray and meditate on the Stations of the Cross, it isn't simply to remember Jesus' suffering 2,000 years ago. It also unites our present suffering with his and gives our suffering meaning. More importantly, it connects us to Christ who suffers today in the least of our brothers and sisters. Together we show God is present with us here and now.

LIFE WITHOUT FATHER

My father and I never quite saw eye to eye. I had the suspicion each of us harbored the unspoken fear we were not measuring up to the other's expectations. It was only in the last years of his life, when he was an Alzheimer's patient in a nursing home, that I finally learned what he thought of me, not just as a priest but also as his son.

In the beginning of his illness, while he still lived at home, we thought we could care for him. At first his memory lapses seemed amusing, but later they became alarming. By the time we decided we could no longer care for him, he had become dangerous. He would argue loudly with my sister to move her car so he could get his out of the driveway. He would get up in the middle of the night, put an empty pot on the stove, turn on the gas and then go back to bed. My poor mother was beside herself trying to follow him around all the time and keep him out of harm's way.

In the nursing home, he recognized us at first and always wanted to go home. Then he asked us for money so the nurses wouldn't kill him. One day my sister handed him some Xeroxed copies of money in hopes of placating him. He looked at the bogus bills, looked at her and said, "What are you, nuts?" One time he told me, "I recognize your voice but your nose is wrong." It wasn't long before such amusing exchanges ceased.

As his memory faded, he no longer recognized us. When we told him who we were, he'd apologize and cry. Then a few minutes later he'd ask us again who we were. I started wearing my Roman collar when I visited him, to give him a familiar sight to help jog his memory. He mistook me for a local pastor. "Where are you from, Father?" he'd say. When I told him I was his son, Joe, he'd start to cry again, so after a while I just said I was a missionary.

Then one day he told me he had a son who was also a missionary and how proud he was of him working in Korea. He asked if I'd ever heard of Father Joe Veneroso or of Maryknoll. I said, "Yes."

"He's going up and up," he said. "My son."

I felt a strange mix of emotions. While I was certainly happy to finally hear he was proud of me, I was also sad because he didn't realize I was his son visiting him. And I was angry because now I had no way to make peace with him before he died.

Maybe that's why I feel ambivalent about Father's Day each year. Now at least I can skip the obligatory card in which I hid my true feelings behind words by Hallmark. Even though my father died in 1991, every Father's Day I still mourn, not so much for him but for a relationship that I never had and that might have been.

Ironically, it was easier for me to travel half way around the world and learn Korean to speak the good news to strangers than it was for the first 21 years of my life to walk across the room and talk heart-to-heart with my Dad.

I share this story with you in hopes of inspiring some of you to swallow your pride before it's too late. Now is the time to make that longest of journeys—across the great generational divide—before it's too late.

SEEING I-TO-I

Every three years while serving on overseas mission we Maryknoll missioners were given a one-month furlough to come back home and visit family. My being away for so long was rougher on my aging parents than on me, but staying a whole month at home seemed a long time for me, who wanted to get back to mission work. I made it a practice to visit homebound parishioners of St. Michael's parish in my hometown of Amsterdam, N.Y., and bring them Holy Communion. When I looked at the list of patients I immediately recognized one name: Ignazio "Mike" Rolando. My parents used to drag me over to his house when I was a boy. As they all sat in the kitchen and chatted away in Italian, I sat there twiddling my thumbs and counting the black and white checks on the tablecloth. I never learned the mother tongue as a kid and it would be years until I majored in Italian in college.

In the years since then I learned Mike had suffered a stroke and was now confined to a wheelchair. He had been my father's "best" friend, but the two had some sort of falling out and hadn't spoken to each other in 11 years. As I entered Mike's home, I smiled when I saw the black and white checkered tablecloth in the kitchen. I approached Mike in his wheelchair. *"Sono il figlio di Valentino,"* I said in Italian. "I am Valentino's son."

He took my hand and pressed it to his lips. His eyes welled up. "Why doesn't your father come to see me anymore?" he asked. I just shook my head.

Back home I told my Dad, "I saw Mike Rolando today." When my father made absolutely no response, I moved in closer and pressed, "He wants you to go and visit him."

His silence prompted my mother, ever the diplomat, to

explain, "Mike didn't visit your father when he was in the hospital after his operation."

"That was in 1966!" I said in disbelief.

"I was in the hospital for two weeks," my father said in his own defense. "He had plenty of time to come see me if he wanted to."

"Dad, Mike's had a stroke. He's in a wheelchair and I doubt he gets out of the house. If you ever want to see him again, you . . ."

"Let's stay friends," was my father's why of cutting off the conversation by suggesting I drop it.

But I couldn't resist a parting shot. "Not if this is the way you treat them."

A few days later, I was napping on the couch when my father shook me awake. "Come on," he said, "Let's go see Mike." The fondest memory I have of my father occurred later that afternoon when we both walked into Mike's house. My father knelt beside the wheelchair to bring himself eye-to-eye with his friend. I don't recall any words being said, but I remember two (no, make that three) grown men crying.

"Reconcile" has an interesting root: *Cilium* is Latin for "eyelash." Con, of course, means "with" and re means "again." Reconciliation requires both parties have the humble strength to kneel, if that is required, in order to see eye-to-eye once again.

As a foreign missioner, I am supposed to bring Christ's gospel of reconciliation to people living at the ends of the earth. I worked 12 years in Korea and have visited more than 19 countries, but sometimes I think my most effective mission work was accomplished one summer afternoon just a few blocks from home.

MONSTERS IN OUR MIDST

They wear bizarre clothes, speak a strange, undecipherable language and are known to prowl in herds ranging in numbers between three and 10,000. What is this menace? A newly discovered species? Sci-fi monsters? Invaders from outer space? Worse. You know them by the far more intimidating term: teenagers.

Anthropologists insist we adults evolved from teenagers and some of us may even be related to them. Given that, it's amazing how little we adults actually know about today's teenagers or how little we are able to communicate with them. Or they with us.

In my more than 20 years working with Korean American teenagers, who do not differ all that much from their all-American counterparts, I have learned that they will put up with just about anything from adults, including incessant reminders of how different and, of course, better things were "Back in my day . . ." They will put up with a lot from us, but will not, however, brook insincerity. They can determine in a nanosecond if we are speaking out of concealed contempt, power plays or genuine concern.

Paradoxically, while teenagers resent being told what to do, at the same time they appreciate learning what is right and wrong—and perhaps more importantly, why. "Because I said so" never cut it with us when we were young; why do we suppose it will with them?

Arbitrary rules lead eventually to the breaking of legitimate laws arbitrarily. We can forbid teenagers to smoke and thus increase the chances they will join the ranks of nicotine addicts who began by sneaking a smoke behind our backs. Or we can honestly share with them our fear of losing them to lung cancer and emphysema. Teenagers are programmed to rebel, like clockwork. They may feel compelled to challenge the limits we impose but they seldom intentionally betray our trust. They'd much rather anger us than hurt us, or worse, disappoint us. Their days are filled with adults talking to them, at them, or about them—just like this! They long for just one adult whom they can to talk to and trust, someone who knows their situation but does not judge, who learns about their fears but does not laugh, who might not share their dreams but does not belittle or dismiss them.

The best examples in maturity we can offer youth is to be fair at all times, even when life isn't, to respect their opinions and feelings, even when we don't agree or understand them. Adults make the mistake of presuming we know what teenagers think, feel, hope or fear, and therefore need, just because we were once teenagers. But to quote the intro to the famous Star Wars series, that was "long, long ago in a galaxy far, far away." The only effective way to learn why modern teenagers think and act the way they do is to ask them. They are in the uncomfortable position of straddling both the adult world and childhood. It would be a mistake to force them to grow up too fast; at the same time they require a benevolent introduction into the mature and rather daunting adult world of responsibilities, integrity and healthy relationships. Ultimately, like it or not, we are the role models responsible for how our teenagers turn out. It has been that way since the beginning of time. If adults learn to listen more and judge less, we'll realize teenagers are not such monsters after all.

9.
Suffering, Death and Dying

DEATH AND STUFF LIKE THAT

Growing up as the son of Italian immigrants, I assumed people everywhere responded to death the same way we did. According to my parents, in the "old days" women wore black for long periods of mourning. Wakes, usually held in the home, lasted for days and a huge meal followed the Requiem Mass. Back in the Old Country, grave plots were not bought, but rented for 10 years, after which the bones were collected, washed and stored in the parish basement. When I went to college and got to meet people of other ethnic backgrounds, I was surprised to hear that other nationalities seldom heard of "jumpers"— mourners who fling themselves into an open grave during the funeral. Most modern American funerals seem boring and bland by comparison—except, perhaps, for the famous jazz send-offs of New Orleans.

Overseas, death is not so easily dismissed. It is an integral part of life. A traditional Korean wake is just that: mourners stay awake until the burial, three or more days later. While things have changed somewhat in Seoul and the larger cities, when I was there Korea had few mortuaries. Relatives washed and dressed the body themselves. Many Catholic parishes have special groups of volunteers who offer this service. Tradition called for mourners to wail nonstop until the burial. In recent years a tape recording of wailing fulfills this obligation. Men often pass the time outside in the courtyard where a special tent had been erected. There they eat, drink and play cards all night long. Embalming or using anything other than a wooden coffin strikes Koreans as being unnatural. In fact, the gravediggers sprinkle lime on the coffin to ensure the quick return to the earth of it and its contents.

Nepal has the most fascinating—if not bizarre by Western standards—funeral practice. With arable land at a premium, the Nepalese cannot afford the luxury of cemeteries. Instead, the remains of the loved one are "prepared" and placed on high funeral towers in the open air for the winged spirits (vultures) to come and carry off to the heavens.

From the mundane to the macabre, humans have dealt with death in a variety of ways over the centuries. Most reflect some belief in an afterlife. Foreknowledge of our own ultimate and inevitable demise distinguishes our species. Humans cultivated religion and philosophy to grapple with the meaning of life and the ever-present shadow of death. Most made connections between what happens after we die with the purpose of life. For millennia tyrants and dictators exploited the fear of death to intimidate and control the people.

The Roman Empire was no different. In fact, they perfected the art of cruelty to maintain control. Except one day in A.D. 33, the Empire played its death card once too often. Sweating blood, Jesus nonetheless faced death head on. By doing so, he set us free, not from physical death, but from the far more paralyzing fear of death, which prevents us from living and loving fully and freely. Death will always remain the most terrible and frightening of mysteries, for which there is no solution and from which there is no escape. Customs, ceremonies and rituals around the world attest to its dominant place in the human psyche. As people of faith in the Crucified and Risen Lord, Christians can only bless death as "our sister," like St. Francis did. We see it as a natural, albeit scary, part of creation and trust in the even greater mystery of love and life we receive from the hand of God.

OUR DISASTROUS GOD

God has a lot to answer for. It's hard enough to convince people there is a God. But we not only proclaim God exists, but also that God created and rules the universe. God is all-powerful, we insist. God is all-loving and all-merciful. God created humans in the divine image. God loves us and became one of us in Jesus Christ. Then one day the earth quakes, a tornado tears across a town, a volcano erupts or a tsunami sweeps away thousands of people and leaves countless others with shattered lives. Among the wreckage: our pathetically inadequate theology. Where was our almighty, all-merciful God then? One wonders.

Theology, I maintain, results when what we believe rubs up against the rough and ragged edges of reality. Reality smashed into all belief systems on December 26, 2004, when a monster tsunami killed more than 200,000 in Thailand and around Southeast Asia, leaving unspeakable carnage and a stunned humanity in its wake. The wave destroyed everything and everyone in its path, with no deference to nationality, religion, age, gender or race. People of various faiths still struggle to understand why.

When something disastrous like this happens, Hindus point to Shiva, the god of destruction; Buddhists, the law of karma.

Muslims, by definition, submit to the will of Allah. Jews find solace in Isaiah's account of the Suffering Servant as well as the story of Job. This time, all religious explanations failed to satisfy. Atheists have it easiest: the earth sometimes quakes, tsunamis sometimes happen and innocent people, if they are in the wrong place at the wrong time, get killed. Period. No God = no dilemma.

And still people suffer, whether they believe in God or not. As Catholics we cling to the cross of Christ, not as a solution to suffering, much less protection from it, but as a response to it. We cry out with our crucified Savior, "My God, my God, why have you forsaken me?" (Matt. 27:46). In spite of it all, we believe. We answer the mystery of suffering with the equally inscrutable mystery of love. When something terrible happens, after asking the unanswerable, "Why?" the best in human nature asks, "What?"—as in, "Now that this has happened, what can I do to help?" The human family, believers and non-believers alike, poured out their compassion in historic proportions upon the tsunami survivors, proving that, despite our differences—religious, economic, ethnic or racial—we are all one family on Earth. It is a timely, albeit costly, lesson.

Brother John Beeching revealed a hidden, more tragic side to the Thailand tsunami. He and Father Mike Bassano spent four days in Phuket, Thailand, assisting Burmese and Mon refugees from Myanmar. As many as 4,000 of them died in the tsunami, but because so many were in Thailand illegally, survivors were not allowed to register lost family members or claim bodies. Fearing deportation, an estimated 30,000 people fled into the hills following the tsunami and remained without access to food, water or medical supplies. Answering the challenge, "What can I do to help?" the missioners brought food to some 324 refugee families hiding in the forest.

Among God's many gifts to us, the most awesome—and scary—is free will. Disasters happen. No one knows why. People suffer. Everywhere. Every day. The poor, the sick, the lonely, the elderly and the oppressed deserve compassion, whether they live next-door or half a world away. We have been blessed with so much. What are we doing to help? We have a lot to answer for.

BLESSED MOURNING

What is so blessed about mourning? Of all the Beatitudes, "Blessed are they who mourn" seems most baffling, if not contradictory. In some translations, it's stranger still. "Blessed" is rendered as "happy." How can we mourn and be happy at the same time? It seems oxymoronic.

Mourning has fallen out of fashion in modern America. Time was when strict norms dictated mourning times and customs. For people of European ancestry, black was the proper color for mourning a spouse or parent, and not just during the funeral. Dressing all in black for anything less than six months was considered scandalous and disrespectful. After that, one could "break mourning" with a touch of white, gradually working up to an outfit of somber grey.

People did not attend social functions or go to the movies while in deep mourning. They resisted the temptation to pretend things were normal to let the realization set in that the definition of normal had forever changed. Their loved one was gone for good.

Such austere practices served a practical purpose. They shielded mourners from the demands of daily social interactions and distractions, thus giving their hearts and minds sufficient time to heal. Nowadays, in our rush to get back to life as "usual" much has been lost, not the least of which is our mental health.

Nowadays we view death as a rude interruption. People may try to comfort small children at the loss of a pet by too quickly replacing it with another one. The story is told of one well-meaning mother who tried to console her child over the death of the family cat by telling her not to cry because God took it. Stunned, the child turned to the mother and said, "What does God want with a dead cat?"

Worse, in their eagerness to shield the child from the sorrow that naturally follows a death of a pet, parents may too soon try to replace it with another. Denied a chance to grieve properly, the child is also deprived of the emotional opportunity to grow. He or she learns the erroneous lesson that the pain of loss is merely an inconvenience to be avoided and, worse, that pets and even people are interchangeable.

Such dismissals do not, in fact, rejuvenate life but, slowly, almost inperceptively, deaden it. More things than death need grieving. A failed marriage, a lost job, an unsuccessful college application, all demand we admit some doors have closed to us forever. When we take time to mourn the inevitable loss of youth, health and even our dreams, we honor them in order to let them go and let us go on. We do not live fully by pretending life has no limits. In fact, experience shows that often we do our best when pressing against our limitations, which force us to concentrate our time and efforts.

The cross compels us to become fully alive not by avoiding pain and loss but by passing through them. The cross, and by extension death, is the ultimate limitation. Every November, All

Souls Month, the Church encourages us to remember those who have died. This is in no way morbid or picking open old wounds. Rather, we bless the emptiness created by their passing. Towards the end of the month we gather to give thanks, not just for what we have but also for what we once had and which is now gone forever. In allowing ourselves a time to mourn, we expand our capacity to love and live and, in so doing, become truly blessed and, yes, happy.

THE FIRST STATION: JESUS IS CONFINED TO A NURSING HOME

Koreans tell the story of a family who cared for an elderly grandfather for many years. Eventually he could no longer handle chopsticks or feed himself, so all his food was mixed together in an old wooden bowl. After the old man died, his son threw the bowl away. To his surprise, his little boy ran to retrieve it from the garbage can. "Do you want to keep that bowl to remember Grandfather by?" he asked.

"No," the boy said nonchalantly, "I'm keeping it for when you get old."

Times are changing even in Korea. Respect for the elderly, once a hallmark of Korean society, cannot resist the changes imposed by modern living. More nuclear families live in small apartments in high-rise dwellings in the sprawling cities rather than several generations of extended families living on family homesteads in country villages. In years past, it was not uncommon for three generations to live together under one roof. Nowadays, cramped quarters barely accommodate parents and one child, let alone "extra" family members. I used to think once I got old, I'd love to live my golden years in Korea. Now, even that "Elderly Paradise" is fast disappearing.

Once, while I was visiting a nursing home here in the States and bringing Catholic residents the Blessed Sacrament, an elderly woman sitting in the hall called me over. I thought she just wanted to talk or perhaps ask me for a prayer or blessing. She drew me near and I bent down to hear her frail voice. "Jesus had it easy," she told me. "His crucifixion was over in three hours." Her words might seem blasphemous were they not uttered by a woman racked with pain who had been confined to a wheelchair for many years. She had a point. Through her and countless others like her, Jesus was bearing the cross of old age.

Remember when living to an advanced age was once considered a blessing? New treatments and discoveries in modern medicine have certainly extended our life span. But social standards have not kept up. Busy schedules and individual priorities have shunted the elderly aside. For many people today, old age has become their personal Way of the Cross. Like Jesus, they suffer abandonment, misunderstanding and, tragically, sometimes mistreatment, hostility and even violence. In a society that caters to and almost idolizes youth and productivity, old age and its accompanying infirmities and illnesses have become a curse. Perhaps, like the father of the boy with the bowl, we resent being reminded that old age has less to do with our past than with our future.

We urgently need role models of how to grow old, if not gracefully, then at least courageously. In Albany, N.Y., I had the privilege of meeting Sr. Louise Principe. Confined by muscular dystrophy to a wheelchair, she started a new religious community for people like her with visible handicaps. There were only two other requirements: members had to support themselves with outside jobs and they also had to volunteer their services by helping the local Church. Sister Louise actually helped form and minister to the Korean Catholic community in the capital district years before they were able to have their own priest.

She points out that Jesus did his greatest work of salvation when he, like her, was "paralyzed" on the cross, unable to move his arms or legs. Sr. Louise and countless other handicapped people challenge us to rethink our attitudes toward sickness and old age, and to be thankful for what we can still do with what we still have.

10.
Peace and Justice

MAKING THE POOR GO AWAY

In 1995 a full-page ad appeared in the *New York Times* showing a wood carving of a classic image of Jesus, halo and all, with the words: "How can you worship a homeless man on Sunday and ignore him on Monday?" This appeal from a coalition for the homeless strikes to the heart of Christianity. It must have made an impression on me, as I remember it to this day.

From "Blessed are the poor" (Luke 6:20) to "Whatsoever you do to the least of my brothers and sisters, you do to me" (Matt. 25:40), the true measure of holiness and faith for the Catholic has always been how our professed love of God translates into action as love of our neighbor, not the number of novenas we make, nor rosaries we say.

Those old enough to recall the War on Poverty in the 1960s and then Hands Across America in 1986 may be surprised or perhaps discouraged to learn that, in a bizarre fulfillment of Jesus' words, the poor we will always have with us (Matt. 26:11). But in the popular mind, the War on Poverty seems to have been replaced by a war on the poor themselves. They're poor because they are lazy, we are told, unwilling to work, unwashed and unwanted. We may even attribute these to entire groups or races of people. Sadder still, some Catholics concur.

When we recall the War on Poverty, or Hands Across America,

or the 1996 International Year to Eradicate Poverty, and look at the poverty here and around the world, it's easy to get discouraged. We tend to react much the same way as the disciples did when Jesus told them to feed the hungry multitude from their meager resources (Matt. 14:16). Why, we barely have enough for ourselves, we protest, let alone enough for those people. Make them go away, we beg. We have yet to learn that making a problem invisible not only is not a solution, but also ultimately makes the situation worse.

Interestingly enough, we do not need another miracle of the multiplication of loaves and fishes to eradicate poverty. Americans waste enough food every day to feed every man, woman and child in the world for three days. Some years ago dairy farmers poured their milk down drains rather than send it to market because the price of milk no longer made it profitable. These days many farmers have switched from growing wheat for food to growing corn for ethanol fuel. This had contributed to food shortages around the world and threatens to lead to wide-spread unrest. We have the resources, but we lack the resolve. Christ showed us the Way, but we lack the will.

To be fair, Catholics have a well-deserved reputation for responding to the needs of the poor with generosity and true Christian charity. Yet more often, we find it easier to help poor individuals in need, or make donations to organizations that help individuals in need rather than ask the hard, uncomfortable questions, make necessary changes in our lifestyle and join in the struggle to uproot the unjust causes of poverty once and for all. As the parable of the widow's mite teaches, we give little when we give from our abundance (Mark 12:43). True faith compels us to give from our need.

The initial question posed by the *Times* ad remains valid. How can we worship a homeless man on Sunday and ignore him the rest of the week? When we ignore the poor and the homeless, we ignore Christ himself.

PATRIOTS AND PROPHETS

Over the years, U.S Catholics have been blessed with freedom of religion. When the Roman Catholic Church and the United States of America share common goals, they form a powerful and mutually supportive partnership. Occasionally, however, the government takes a position that directly violates Church teaching, such as it did when it legalized abortion. Then there is the controversial and divisive case of the war in Iraq. The pope unequivocally condemned this war. Can a Catholic American oppose U.S. policy without being labeled a traitor? Can an American Catholic take exception to the official Church position without being treated like a heretic?

No institution can escape human weakness and sinfulness. Over the centuries our Church has made serious missteps, such as the Inquisition and the Crusades. The United States, too, adopted inhumane policies it later regretted and was forced to abolish, such as the mistreatment of Native Americans, slavery, racial segregation and the internment of Japanese-Americans during World War II.

Institutions, be they religious or political, tend to resist making changes voluntarily. Thus, it took prophetic witnesses such as St. Francis of Assisi, St. Teresa of Avila and St. Ignatius of Loyola to spark spiritual revolutions that called the Church away from corruption and back to gospel basics. Similarly, Susan B. Anthony, Rosa Parks and Martin Luther King Jr. displayed down-to-earth patriotism that challenged our nation to live up to its promises set forth in the Declaration of Independence that "all . . . are created equal . . ."

We need both patriots and prophets if the United States and the Roman Catholic Church are to survive, much less improve. Flying a flag and wearing a flag lapel pin are easy and not at all indicative of true patriotism. How about voting? Serving jury duty? Paying your fair share of taxes? Writing a letter to the editor? Visiting your congressional representatives to express support or opposition to proposed legislation? Petitioning the government, be it local, state or federal, for the redress of grievances? Marching in a demonstration to oppose U.S. policy, whether it is abortion or war? Defending someone else's right to express an opinion, even when it disagrees with yours? Surely these actions flow from the heart of someone who really loves this country and understands what it means to be an American.

Similarly, our Church badly needs prophets in these dark days of disillusionment following the sex abuse and authority abuse scandals. Is the answer to take a serious look and hold an indepth conversation about modern human sexuality and the addictive nature of power, or to silence all dissent and focus efforts on returning to the centralized, top-down unquestioning approach prevalent before the reforms of the Second Vatican Council? Prophets are people brave enough to risk official sanctions in order to speak truth to power and, by their words and lives, make us all feel uneasy. Their examples create controversy as they prick our collective conscience. They remind us of a more noble life God calls us to live and warn of the disastrous consequences should we stubbornly refuse to mend our ways. Prophets risk ridicule, imprisonment, censorship, silencing and sometimes death to be true to the gospel.

We must avoid the temptation to vilify the true prophets and patriots in our midst. Without them, both church and country are doomed. With them, greater days lie ahead.

STOP KILLING KIDS

J esus loved and blessed children (Matt. 19:14) but what else would you expect from a bachelor? He never lost sleep with their 2:00 a.m. feedings, colic, wetting and whining. He didn't worry himself sick when they stayed out late as teenagers. He never had to tell them a million times to clean their rooms, wipe their feet, eat their vegetables and do their homework. He didn't have to worry about what kind of friends they were hanging out with or what impact society's skewed morality would have on them. And what thanks do parents get for all their work, worry and sacrifice to bring another life into this world? An in-your-face "I never asked to be born." It's far easier to resent children, especially someone else's. Perhaps that's why Jesus blessed them.

Even the United States, arguably the richest nation not just in the world but also in all human history, does not place a very high priority on its children, lofty political rhetoric aside. Those children fortunate enough to avoid getting aborted, abandoned or abused still face a dubious future of hunger, disease and neglect. Drugs, tobacco and alcohol claim many. The situation is even worse for minority children. When our economy takes a downturn, the poor suffer most. Children's health programs get vetoed even as more and more money goes into war that, in turn, surely negatively impacts the lives of children overseas. Congress reports one out of four children in the United States lives below the poverty level and goes to bed hungry, even with both parents working. A growing percentage of our nation's homeless population is children. Runaways gravitate towards big-city life—and death. Street kids lose what innocence they had to prostitution, gangs and violent crime.

This phenomenon is by no means peculiar to the United States but rather is endemic to many modern, industrialized nations. To rid society of dangerous criminal elements, some countries have resorted to killing street children, notorious for committing crimes and growing up as hardened criminals. Killing unwanted street children seems an extreme yet logical extension of an abortion mentality. After all, why should society have to put up with someone else's unwanted children? They'll only propagate more unwanted children, and at an earlier age. We would not hesitate, the argument goes, to exterminate plague-infested rats or virus-infected chickens. Besides, "exterminate" sounds so negative. Think of it as post-natal population control or, better, pre-emptive crime prevention.

Alarmed by the anti-child mentality prevalent in the United States, the U.S. bishops have long challenged politicians to consider the impact of laws and policies on the welfare of children. Tragically, the sex abuse scandals that exploded upon the Church in the United States seriously eroded the bishops' moral authority to speak on behalf of children. To their credit, the bishops publicly and repeatedly apologized for their role and complicity in the scandal. They began a long and painful process to re-examine their own policies and attitudes. Today, Catholic dioceses of the United States lead the way in advocating true child protection. The bishops call on all Americans to help create a safe, nurturing and welcoming world where parents, and especially mothers, feel supported in their decision to have children and where all children find love, safety and blessings.

VIOLENCE STOPS HERE

From the musical *Fiddler On the Roof* comes the folksy wisdom, "An eye for an eye, a tooth for a tooth and soon everyone will be blind and toothless." From the most ancient Hammurabi's Code, the "Eye for an eye" law was in fact an attempt to curtail vengeance, not administer it. Thus, if someone caused a neighbor to lose an eye, the victim could not demand two eyes, much less a life or limb, in retribution.

Jesus sought to break the vicious cycle of violence and revenge by telling his followers to turn the other cheek (Matt. 5:39). He commanded us to love our enemies and pray for those who persecute us. Then, from the cross, he showed us how by asking the Father to forgive his executioners. Still, the urge to seek revenge and the desire to fight injustice is almost irresistible, especially when defending the weak or those we love.

That being said, we can see a seeming contradiction in Jesus' life. Called "Prince of Peace," Jesus also said, "I come not to bring peace, but the sword" (Matt. 10:34). He recognized his followers would face violent opposition and death if they put his words into practice. Overcome with righteous indignation, Jesus reacted violently against the property of the moneychangers when he saw how they were desecrating the only place in the Temple precinct where Gentiles were allowed to worship (Matt. 21:12).

It comes as no surprise that Christians are likewise conflicted over whether it is morally right to resort to violence or go to war. Throughout the ages, Christians have espoused everything from nonviolence to the "just war" theory. The early Church forbade Christians from serving in the military, not so much because of the violence as it was to avoid idolatry: the emperor was divine and soldiers knelt before his image. Today we have chaplains of all religious backgrounds bravely serving the men and women in our armed forces. At the same time we have Christians invoking their faith as a reason to be conscientious objectors. Pacifists invoke Francis of Assisi. Combatants look to Joan of Arc.

It is hardest to witness to the gospel of peace in the midst of a violent situation. For more than 20 years Sudanese Catholics have been targeted as the enemy alongside their animist neighbors by an Islamic regime bent on imposing *Sharia,* or Muslim law, on the whole country. Medical personnel in Cambodia try to rehabilitate amputees wounded by "leftover" landmines from a war that supposedly ended decades ago. Missioners in Mozambique pick up the shattered lives from that country's long war for independence followed by a brutal civil war. People of faith in the Philippines search for ways to bridge the widening gulf between warring Christian and Muslim factions.

Perhaps the greatest example of Christian nonviolence and forgiveness followed the terrible shooting of ten Amish schoolgirls in October 2006 by a deranged gunman, who then took his own life. The shocked, tightly knit Amish community included the soul of the gunman in their prayers. What's more, the funeral cortege of horse-drawn buggies also stopped by the house of the gunman's widow and the community shared with her the donations that poured in with condolences. The nation, the world took notice.

There is no "one size fits all" solution. Only those involved in a situation can best determine the most gospel-centered response. The greatest temptation facing the conscientious Christian is the desire to do whatever it takes to stop one group from hurting another. The greatest evil would be to do nothing.

TIRED WOLF OR BRAVE LAMB?

The prophet Isaiah paints a wonderful picture of peaceful Messianic times when the "wolf shall lie down with the lamb" (Isa. 11:6) Comedian Woody Allen commented that this may come to pass, but "the lamb won't get much sleep." Is Isaiah's vision an unrealistic pipedream, or is there hope for reconciliation among natural enemies?

A Korean legend from the sixteenth century tells of an actual "wolf and lamb" encounter between an invading Japanese general and a "conquered" Buddhist monk. Undisturbed by the battle raging outside the monastery, the monk continued in deep meditation. Intrigued, the general interrupted him, saying, "Swine! Look at me! What do you see?"

The monk took a moment to slowly open his eyes and gaze at his would-be tormenter. "I see the Lord Buddha," he said.

"That's strange," the general sneered. "When I look at you I see only a pig."

That serene smile of enlightenment crossed the monk's face. This seemed to unsettle the general a bit. "That's no surprise," the monk said. "For the one who has the Buddha's heart looks out upon the world with Buddha's eyes and therefore sees Buddha in all things, while the one who has the heart of a pig looks out on the world with the eyes of a pig and . . ."

The story doesn't say what happened next. Did this wolf lie down with the lamb or devour him? No matter, the wolf lost! The lamb triumphed, not by force or compromising ideals but by recognizing something holy even in his adversary. The lamb challenged the wolf to have a change of heart. Was the pacifist monk capable of doing something the warrior could not?

At baptism, we also undergo a spiritual change of heart.

Without this rebirth, what hope do we have of keeping the commandments, much less of following Christ? God implants in us the heart of the true Lamb who takes away the sins of the world. It enables us to recognize Jesus in the least of our brothers and sisters—even in those who hate us and would do us harm. Still, human nature being what it is, even Christians sometimes find forgiveness and reconciliation difficult.

On December 2, 1980, members of the Salvadoran army killed four U.S. Churchwomen. Two were Maryknoll Sisters, one an Ursuline nun and the fourth a lay missioner from Cleveland. We struggle to forgive the soldiers who did this as well as the officers who gave the orders to carry out the cowardly act. We also try to find it in our hearts to forgive the U.S. government officials who deliberately lied about these rapes and murders, as well as the School of the Americas in Fort Benning, Georgia, where so many other human rights abusers from Latin America were trained over the years. Forgiveness is especially difficult when those responsible deny all guilt, remain in power and continue in their duplicity. Without justice, without an investigation and full disclosure, or at least an admission of guilt, amnesty only mocks the memory of those who died. Still we recognize the need to forgive for our own sakes. An adage in the Twelve Step program warns us: "Resentment is a poison we drink in hopes our enemy will die."

Yes, the heart of Christ within us impels us to look upon our enemies and recognize the image of God. Yet even as the forgiveness of Christ calls us to repentance, our capacity to forgive challenges our enemies to a change of heart. Let the wolf know the lamb can roar.

THANK GOD IT'S NOT OUR HALF OF THE BOAT THAT'S SINKING

I once saw a political cartoon in which the nations of the world were depicted as passengers fleeing an obviously sinking ship. (Read: terrorist threats, ecological disaster, international debt, overpopulation or globalization, etc.) As the survivors huddled aboard a small lifeboat, their dire situation worsens when their boat springs a serious leak. One naive passenger tries to reassure the others by pointing out, "Don't panic, folks. It's not our half of the boat that's sinking."

We are all aboard the Good Ship Planet Earth together. Nothing happens to one part of Earth that doesn't affect all of us. We cannot ignore a crisis half a world away thinking it has no impact on our lives. In this day of instant communication and global travel and commerce, we cannot afford to ignore our neighbor's problems, even if it's for the selfish motive of protecting ourselves.

We can point a finger at Latin American farmers for growing the coca leaves that get turned into cocaine that winds up on our streets and ensnares our fellow citizens in drug addiction. But if we make no effort to curtail addiction here in the United States and help addicts, or help farmers south of the border to replace coca plants with other less profitable but legitimate and healthy crops, we can expect more drug-related deaths and violent crime in our country. If we continue to justify selling weapons to less than democratic regimes, we increase the very risk of war and instability we had hoped to contain. We end up exacerbating the very menace we helped to create. Case in point: To thwart the Soviet Union's attempt to occupy Afghanistan during the 1980s, the C.I.A. heavily armed the Mujahadeen (so-called "Freedom

Fighters") with billions of dollars of weapons. The Russians withdrew in defeat. The Soviet Union subsequently collapsed. But the Taliban took over Afghanistan and the most famous Mujahadeen, Osama bin Laden, organized Al-Qaeda and set up headquarters there from which they planned the September 11 attacks on the United States.

As the debate over illegal immigrants in this country rages, we forget that the hijackers of those planes that slammed into the Twin Towers, the Pentagon and the field in Pennsylvania were all here legally. Invoking homeland security as a pretext to capture, detain and deport people does not get to the root of the question as to why they are here in the first place. Closing our borders (and minds) to refugees may be easier, but more dangerous in the long run, than dealing with the negative impact U.S. policies have on the economies of these countries, thus forcing more and more of their people to come here to find work. The North American Free Trade Agreement (NAFTA) not only outsourced many American jobs, it undermined Mexican businesses thus exacerbating an already serious problem.

As Catholics and Americans, we have a double duty: to be true to the gospel and loyal to our country. We can serve both Church and State by learning all we can about people in other parts of the world and sharing our information with our fellow citizens, especially our elected officials. When we foster the idea that all people on Earth are our brothers and sisters for whom our faith compels us to show concern, we exhibit the finest qualities of Catholicism and the United States. By cultivating a truly "catholic," that is universal, worldview, we can plug the leaks of apathy, prejudice and racism that threaten to sink us all.

WHOSE GOD REIGNS?

Religion and money have a lot in common. Both come in a variety of denominations. We argue about them. They bring value to our lives. People die—and kill—for them. Try as we might, we can't get away from either of them. Paradoxically, money and religion need each other. You might say there is an unholy alliance, or rather, a marriage of convenience between the two.

Religion needs money to carry out its good works, not to mention purchase all the trappings that go into worship services. U.S. money says, "In God We Trust" on it and currency requires people put faith in its worth. While we deal with them on a daily basis, religious and money matters sometimes seem incomprehensible to the very people who need and use them most. Ordinary people, priests included, might find a theological explanation of the Holy Trinity as perplexing as an economist's speech about how the dollar's devaluation impacts our national debt. I still remember as a boy asking Sister Jane Marie what God did during that whole eternity prior to creation. "That's a mystery of our faith," she replied and we all genuflected. Of course, these days if you ask a politician or economist who is responsible for the sub-prime mortgage fiasco, you get pretty much the same response.

Sister Jane was not trying to duck the issue by invoking faith but merely conceding that certain truths about God lie totally beyond human ability to understand. Some economists are banking—quite literally—on our inability to comprehend the far-reaching implications of what may yet turn into a more than trillion dollar debacle. One problem, of course, is the sheer amount of money involved. To visualize $1 trillion, imagine a stack of

$100 bills 228 miles high. This time nobody is genuflecting, but we have been brought to our knees.

For good or ill, religion and money both play a role in politics. The major issues of our day—war, abortion, human rights, global warming, racism, sexism and drug abuse, to name a few—all have religious implications since they either enhance or diminish the human person, created, we maintain, in God's image. Unfortunately, when we make decisions, whether informally or in an election, money, not morality, usually casts the deciding vote. People vote more with their pocketbooks than with their prayer books.

Jesus taught that both religion and money must serve humans, not the other way around (Mark 2:27). In our day, Jesus might say, "Religion was made for people, not people for religion." Jesus warns we will be judged by how we used money and religion, to help others or to enslave them. When asked if it was lawful to pay the Temple tax, Jesus recognized this insidious use of money and religion to trap him into making a dangerous choice. If he said pay the tax, the people would lose faith in him, who seemed different from the other religious teachers and who gave them hope for a better world. But if he said don't pay the tax, the authorities could arrest him for inciting rebellion. The coin of tribute belonged to Caesar since it bore the emperor's image. Jesus' answer was more dangerous than their question, for he showed that ultimately we belong to God.

People alone bear God's image. We "render to God the things that are God's" (Matt. 22:21) when all our efforts and resources go toward helping people realize their God-given potential. When Church or State sacrifices people's welfare on the altar of power or expediency, we commit both treason and idolatry.